VENTURING WITH GOD IN CONGO

DARRELL CHAMPLIN

CONJURSKE PUBLICATIONS

2017

The **eternal purpose** of God is to call out from every kindred, tongue, people, and nation a multitude redeemed by the blood of His Lamb slain from the foundation of the world; over whom He will crown His Son, the Lion of the tribe of Judah, King of Kings and Lord of Lords forever. This is

THE PASSION

OF THE HEART OF GOD THAT
CANNOT BE QUENCHED,

THE OBSESSION

OF HIS MIND THAT
CANNOT BE DENIED,

THE VISION

OF HIS EYES FROM ETERNITY PAST INTO
ETERNITY FUTURE THAT WILL NOT DIM, AND

THE DESTINATION

TO WHICH HE HAS COMMITTED HIS
OMNIPOTENT, IMMUTABLE, ETERNAL BEING—

A DESTINATION HE **WILL NOT ABANDON.**

-DARRELL CHAMPLIN ON MISSIONS

ISBN-13: 978-1-935923-04-6

Conjurske Publications

3215 County Rd G

Rhinelander, WI 54501

www.conjurskepublications.com

info@conjurskepublications.com

All Scripture references are taken from the King James Version.

Visit *https://archive.org/details/DarrellChamplin* for a full archive of the author's sermons.

Printed in the United States of America.

CONTENTS

ACKNOWLEDGEMENTS

It is with gratitude to God that we present this account of His good hand upon us to our readers. It has been a family involvement, and we are glad to see it made available to those who have so faithfully fellowshipped with us in the furtherance of the Gospel. Heartfelt thanks goes to the team at Conjurske Publications who have compiled these stories into the fine book that we now send forth. Our prayer is that it may stir your hearts and challenge your minds to serve the God of Heaven Who is so worthy. In the words of Psalm 78:5–7, we seek to make known to the generation to come the works of God, and that our hope is in Him.

Louise Champlin

PRONUNCIATION TIPS
for Lingala

VOWELS:

a	as in	ɑː	*(f<u>a</u>ther)*
e	as in	eɪ	*(s<u>ay</u>)*
i	as in	iː	*(s<u>ee</u>)*
o	as in	oʊ	*(g<u>o</u>)*
u	as in	uː	*(f<u>oo</u>d)*

IRREGULAR SOUNDS:

"N" is pronounced as a nasal sound, with the tongue between the teeth and the roof of the mouth.

Due to the vowel sound this creates, these words are used with the article "an".

(an *N*kai, *N*kole *N*kema)

TIMELINE OF IMPORTANT EVENTS

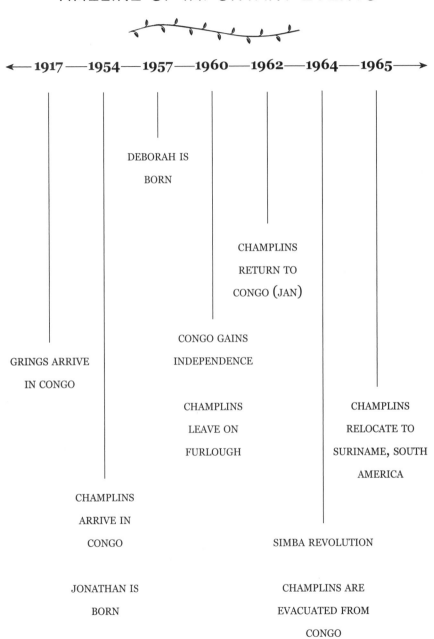

1917 — 1954 — 1957 — 1960 — 1962 — 1964 — 1965

DEBORAH IS

BORN

CHAMPLINS

RETURN TO

CONGO (JAN)

GRINGS ARRIVE

IN CONGO

CONGO GAINS

INDEPENDENCE

CHAMPLINS

LEAVE ON

FURLOUGH

CHAMPLINS

RELOCATE TO

SURINAME, SOUTH

AMERICA

CHAMPLINS

ARRIVE IN

CONGO

SIMBA REVOLUTION

JONATHAN IS

BORN

CHAMPLINS ARE

EVACUATED FROM

CONGO

CONGO

Bunia

Kisangani

Lukenie River

Dekese

Kasai River

Nkole Nkema

Yassa

Kinshasa

Ongo

Ilebo

Longa

Kikwit

Idiofa

Mweka

Kalami

Kananga

Mbuji May

Lubumbashi

INTRODUCTION

AUTOBIOGRAPHICAL SKETCHES

G. DARRELL CHAMPLIN

I was born to George Albert Champlin and Ardath Ivadell Hodgins Champlin in Salt Lake City, Utah on February 22, 1932. As the first boy born in Salt Lake City on the two hundredth anniversary of George Washington, I was awarded a Japanese flowering cherry tree. Planted behind our little adobe brick house at 668 West 2nd North Street, it graced our yard for years, a bright spot in an otherwise dingy neighborhood. Fittingly, it lay between the multi-railed switching yard of the Union Pacific Railroad and the freight line of the Denver and Rio Grande Railroad, whose rails ran down the middle of 7th West Street within half a block of our home. In the winter, freight trains would stop for the red signal ahead, their puffing steam engine dominating the sounds of our night. Then with a chug, the big wheeled iron horse would take up the slack of the couplings between the train cars behind them, the sound of a train gathering itself to move. As boys, we waited for the inevitable spinning of the engine's wheels when they lost their footing on the ice-covered rails. Sometimes such trains would block our way to Jackson School, which lay through the field on the other side of the track.

The foot-thick walls of the squat house in which we lived originally contained a kitchen, bedroom, bath, and combined dining and living room which lay at the front of the house. At a later date, an eight-foot-wide porch had been framed in at the back of the house,

1

creating a bedroom big enough for the bunk bed that my brother Russell and I shared. The only heat available for the cold Utah winters was supplied by an open face unvented natural gas heater located in the living room, always turned off at night. There was no heat in the frame addition. As a result it was common during the winter for my brother and I to awake in the morning and find ice on our blankets where our moist breath had frozen. With some exceptions, our house was a little below the norm for the neighborhood. Our area was a lower-income, older section of town through which Interstate 15 eventually bulldozed its way and buried our house and my flowering cherry tree under an overpass. In contrast, the eastern hillside bank of Salt Lake City was the more affluent neighborhood at that time.

We were neither rich nor poor financially, perhaps, but certainly rich in the things of God, with a Christian father and a deeply spiritual, godly mother of great discernment and power in prayer. My father worked for the Union Pacific Railroad as a boiler maker on steam engines, and laid out for us the principle of hard work by his example.

Our home church, Bethel Baptist, on 9th South and Lincoln Street, was nestled against the slope leading to the east side of town. Somehow our pastor enticed many of the time's great men of God to stop in Salt Lake City on their way to Los Angeles and other points in the west. Folks are astonished when I relate the amazing fact that forty thousand of my generation were called to the mission fields of the world at the average age of ten! Yes, I said ten. My brother Russell, twenty-two months younger than I, was ten when called. I was twelve and can't imagine how it took me so long. When you understand the circumstances of our time, it seems quite natural that we should have been called while young. In those days the heart's desire of godly mothers and fathers was to have the God of Heaven call their sons and daughters to the mission field. That was the crown of the Christian home! Our churches prayed and labored for the same crown: the glory of having young men and women called and sent forth from their own church. No higher honor was imaginable.

You need to know also that there was no junior church in those days. We sat with Mom and Dad in the grown-up services under adult preaching immediately out of the nursery—and we behaved, or else. The result was a group of young boys and girls who at the age of ten had spiritual vocabularies capable of understanding and applying anything they heard from some of the greatest preachers of the day. We were like little Samuels sitting in the temple just waiting to hear the voice of the Spirit of God saying, "I want you for the mission field." Listening Sunday after Sunday to the expository preaching of God's Word, our pastor taught us how to study the Bible for ourselves. Eventually, once the pastor announced his text and exposited his first point, we were already waiting for him at his second and then sitting with anticipation at the verses which would form his conclusion. In our youth department we eagerly launched into the study of the book of Romans. Inflamed with the glory of the Gospel, the excitement was so great that we had to have an "activity." The result was our spontaneous departure from the church to the street corner where we could catch one of the city buses headed to downtown Salt Lake and hold a street meeting preaching the Gospel to lost Mormons. Is it any wonder God called forty thousand such young people as missionaries? A solid foundation on the Word of God produced an abundance of fruit.

At that time in public school, it was possible to participate in what was called the Articulating Unit. This meant that if your grades were high enough through the sixth grade, you were qualified to take the seventh and eighth grades combined in one year. The idea appealed to me, being in a hurry to get to the mission field. This enabled me to enter high school at fourteen and graduate in the summer of my seventeenth year.

Consequently, in September of 1949 I arrived in Los Angeles, California at Fundamental Bible Institute, a school with a strong Bible curriculum. At that time, Tennessee Temple also was a Bible Institute. This was in the midst of the historic Bible Institute movement, which resulted in the greatest missionary outpouring in history.

My training in shorthand and typing served me well, earning me nine dollars a week as secretary to the president of the school, M. H. Reynolds Sr., a well-known western evangelist and fundamentalist.

Over the weekend, we often had preaching assignments in California cities such as Pacific Beach, Portersville, Banning, and Daggett, as well as Las Vegas, Nevada. These provided not only vital experience and training for the mission field, but also the blessing of seeing scores come to Christ in door-to-door soul winning, street preaching, and church services.

Our evangelistic activities also included weekly street meetings on Skid Row, the area of E. 5th and Wall Street in Los Angeles. Eggs and spoiled fruit were thrown from upper story flop house windows, guns were poked into our ribs, and crutches were swung at our heads by broken men with shattered lives. Some verbally regurgitated the rot of their hatred of God and their rebellion against all that is holy. But others—former doctors, executives, and business owners, now dressed in rags reeking with alcohol, their families gone and their lives in tatters—would pour out their hearts in desperate pleas for deliverance and restoration. Miraculously, many of those broken

4

men were mended by our loving Lord. Thus, step by step, the God of Heaven was preparing one of his young servants for the mission field. That preparation extended also to the giving of my life companion and fellow laborer in the harvest fields. At Fundamental Bible Institute I met Louise May Grings, raised in the Belgian Congo of Africa. She has the distinction of being from a family in which most members from 1917 through 2000, including the first two great-grandchildren, have gone to the mission field. Though I was raised in the USA and she on the mission field, we came from a generation that had imbibed a clear vision of the service of God and an undivided determination to follow Him to the ends of the earth, wherever that might be. Thus, we were of one mind and heart in our desire to serve the God of Heaven on the mission field. God brought us together in that mutual purpose, and we were married on June 18, 1951.

In 1954 we started across the USA headed for New York, and ultimately to the "uttermost parts" in obedience to Acts 1:8. With us was our one-year-old son, David, and Louise's brother Mark Grings. I smile when I think of how totally unprepared we were for such an undertaking. Driving a borrowed car, we spoke in the churches with whom we had been associated while in school. Moving out of California, we stopped in Las Vegas where both Mark and I had preached. My home church in Salt Lake City scheduled us for a meeting. Then we were on our way across the USA following the Lincoln Highway. With a meager amount of support raised, we sailed for the Belgian Congo, Africa in June of 1954.

God graciously prospered us with ten productive years of ministry as souls were saved and baptized, churches formed, and faithful men trained as leaders. God also gave us two more children: Jonathan, born the year we arrived, and Deborah, born three years later.

It was a joy venturing with God in the heart of Africa. But unrest surfaced with the advent of independence from Belgium in 1960, civil war broke out in 1964, and that year we were evacuated to the States. At that point, everything we had left in the world fit in two small metal trunks. We fully expected to return as soon as things settled down and the equipment vital to the ministry could be replaced. But our jungle people were scattered, their villages burned, and our mission station destroyed. The government was not allowing any foreigners into the interior, and there was no imminent possibility of returning to our beloved field.

With the door to Congo closed, we were led of God to enter the jungles of Suriname, South America in May 1965. There live the Maroons, descendants of African slaves who revolted against their Dutch masters at about the time of our American Civil War. After a bloody fifty-year conflict, the slaves triumphed and a treaty was made giving them the right to live anywhere in the jungles of Suriname. So these would be "our people", known as Djukas, just in another continent. We came to the field after three missionary families had left due to the suspicious attitudes and distrust of these former slaves' descendants. They wanted nothing to do with the whites who had enslaved them, nor with their god. In December of 1965, we delivered our fourth child and third son, Ethan, as the fourth baby born in our tiny clinic. With God's good hand upon us, we set about being His witnesses the best we knew how, in material, medical, educational, and—most importantly—spiritual service to them. God has allowed us to see the ministry expand, including churches, a Bible institute, clinics, and many evangelistic outreaches in towns and villages. The ministry covers an area of one hundred fifty miles on three different river systems, the east-west highway, the mining town of Moengo, and the capital city, Paramaribo.

Our team in Suriname now includes our three sons, David, Jonathan, and Ethan, and their families, with eleven grandchildren. In our thirty-five years here, God has also given us a doctor and his wife, nurses for our clinics, as well as other families and youth workers. Some of these folks are still on the field; others have retired, gone to glory, or moved to other fields. Happily, we were able to visit Congo in 1988 and since then have made three more trips for evangelism and pastors' conferences. Survivors have rebuilt the destroyed churches. The Grings family was able to return and the number of churches multiplied under their ministry and that of nationals.

IN CONCLUSION, A BRIEF SUMMARY OF OUR USA MINISTRY:

Since 1977, Louise and I have invested about six months each year during spring and fall representing Independent Faith Mission (a fundamental Baptist board) in a variety of Bible Colleges, universities, and churches across the USA. We teach missions as well as help several great missionary churches train their missionaries. Our schedule in the USA also includes preaching for mission "weekends," Sundays, and Wednesdays in approximately forty-five churches. Praise be to God, several hundred of our mission class students are now on the "white unto harvest" fields of the world, as a result of our year being split between the green jungles of the mission field and the asphalt jungles of the USA.

My life verse has been I Corinthians 15:58: "Therefore, my beloved brethren, be ye stedfast, unmoveable, always abounding in the work of the Lord, forasmuch as ye know that your labour is not in vain in the Lord."

7

"It is a good thing to give thanks unto the Lord, and to sing praises unto Thy name, O Most High." (Psalm 92:1)

It is a special joy and privilege for me to share my testimony with you. This verse expresses what I would like to say from my heart. God has been so faithful to me, and I can only thank and praise Him for His good hand upon me.

By His wonderful grace, I was born to Christian parents. That blessing has been a tremendous factor in my life. I grew up with the Word of God as an integral part of everyday living. I came to know the Lord as my personal Savior at the age of six through reading the Gospel of John. My mother always sat with me as I read, and when I reached the account of Christ's sufferings and death on the cross, I was deeply moved.

In tears I asked my mother, "Why did they do that to Him?"

Her answer was wise and to the point: "He died for you!"

I could not let that great sacrifice be in vain. When she directed me back to John 1:12, I responded as the verse indicates we should—"As many as received Him, to them gave He power to become the sons of God, even to them that believe on His name." I received Him and became a child of God that day, which has caused my heart to rejoice ever since.

I was born in 1928 in Lynn Haven, Florida. At the time, my father was helping Bob Jones Sr. on the first campus of Bob Jones College. My folks were missionaries and had begun service in the Belgian Congo in 1917. After 10 years of service, they were in the States for furlough. In 1933 they returned to Congo, so I had the additional opportunity of growing up in what was then the Belgian Congo. My parents were involved with tribal evangelism in the very heart of Africa—a thousand miles of vast tropical jungles surrounding us, and tribe after tribe groping in darkness and the shadow of death. Witch doctors wielded more power and persuasion over the people than the civil authorities, and medical facilities were completely absent. Few survived birth, and many more died young. The drum beating, compulsive dancing, and hysterical death wailing was constantly heard. Literacy was completely absent and blinded eyes were kept in ignorance through fear and superstition imposed by the belief in the ever present *bekadji*—evil spirits and the un-departed spirits of the dead.

Into all of this came our family of seven in 1933. What gives the courage and incentive to face such daunting odds? We had the Gospel—God's power unto salvation! We had the command of God Almighty to "Go!" We had the promise and assurance of the Lord Jesus Christ: "I am with you always." There wasn't an alternative actually; we had to obey! And by the grace of God, our family stayed for thirteen years telling that glorious message of the light, life, liberty, and love of God. And what did God do? We witnessed the pulling down of strongholds and the miracle of the new birth. It was not without a price, however. The family was often beset with the tropical maladies of malaria, dysentery, parasites, and other normal diseases. In all of these things God has His way of moving in a situation to perform His plan, and He did this when we had been there only three years.

He took our mother Home, through malaria that progressed into the more serious black water fever. Without adequate medical facilities there was little we could do to save her life. However, this death of a Christian in their midst turned the tide from idol worship to worshipping the true and living God. A handful became believers, the first fruits of sowing the seed. The corn that fell into the ground did indeed spring up and multiply. Yes, the ten years after my mother's death saw an abundant reaping—fruit that would remain, thank God!

After thirteen years had passed, we children were facing the call to prepare for lifetime service ourselves. Again, we saw God at work in our lives. God's direction is always accompanied by His provision. We were able to return to the States where we received our Bible training. God's provision also included my life companion, Darrell Champlin. In 1954, with our eighteen-month-old son, David, we came back to Congo where I had grown up. What a blessed ten years God gave us in His ripened harvest field! Churches and Christian schools were started and national pastors were trained. God added Jonathan and Debbie to our family as well. But war came in 1964 and we were evacuated.

After a year of waiting in the States and hoping to return to Congo, God opened the door to Suriname, South America. We were in a different continent, but with descendants of former African slaves of the same people group we had worked with in Congo. Living as their ancestors did in Africa, they were without God and in the same bondage of fear and death.

We've been there for over thirty-five years now. God has "added to the church such as should be saved." He also added another son to our family, Ethan. We have watched our children grow up and get their training; our sons have received their God-given helpmates and returned to the field. He gave us eleven grand-children as well.[1] God is so good, and I think you'll understand why I like to "give thanks to the Lord and sing His praises."

Darrell and I now continue on in full time service in three areas: active ministry in Suriname, trips back to Congo since it reopened

---

1   At the time of publishing, there are fifteen grandchildren and six great-grandchildren. See family tree, pg. 12.

to us in 1988, and a representative ministry in churches and Bible colleges in the States for Independent Faith Mission with whom we have served since 1961. What an effective challenge that has been to many young people, who in turn have surrendered their lives to full-time service for the Lord of the Harvest! May this brief account of what God has done encourage and challenge your hearts to trust Him more and purpose to serve Him. To God be the glory!

My life verse: "Being confident of this very thing, that He which hath begun a good work in you will perform it until the day of Jesus Christ." (Philippians 1:6)

...17 YEARS LATER:

These stories were written during the summer and winter months of the year 2000 while we were in Suriname between trips to the states for IFM work. Darrell and I relinquished the representative involvement in 2009 and returned to Suriname full-time. We were blessed to have six more years to invest in the ministry there, till God promoted Darrell to higher service in His presence on August 26, 2015. It has been my privilege to continue working alongside our three sons and their families, doing what I've done all my life. With His enabling, I will continue until He calls me to my eternal Home.

12

LOUISE'S SIBLINGS:

Robert (Bob) & Winifred Grings
(1920–2012 & 1920–1993)
3 Children
9 Grandchildren

Roy & Dorothy Grings
(1922–2006 & 1925–1971)
1 child
4 Grandchildren

John & Bessie Grings Gander
(1926–? & 1925–2010)
2 children
2 Grandchildren

Mark & Wyla Grings
(1931–2008 & 1928–?)
1 Child
6 Grandchildren

Martyred in Congo
Irene Ferrel - Winifred's sister
1921–1964

Elisabeth Louise

Joanna

Rhoda

Priscilla

Silas

Micah

Brynlea

Caleb & Abigail

Alyssa

Kolai Enoch

Seth & Lauren

Nathanael & Hannah

Tabitha

Caleb & Kristen Champlin

Miriam

Deborah Louise Champlin (1957)

Jonathan & Sherrie Champlin (1954 & 1958)

Ethan & Kim Champlin (1965 & 1965)

Talitha

Anna

Lukas Darrell

Matthew & Bethany

David & Lynne Champlin (1952 & 1951)

Dan & Ruthann

Benjamin

G. Darrell Champlin (1932–2015)
Louise Grings Champlin (1928–?)

George Albert Champlin (1909–1970)
Ardath Hodgins Champlin (1912–1980)

Herbert E. Grings (1892–1977)
Ruth Fuller Grings (1888–1936)

MBOMBIANDA

Years before the author arrived in Congo,
his wife's parents lived and worked there.
This is how it began....

The trail was long and seemingly intermi-
nable. Since they had crossed the Kasai River, which
runs east-west through the heart of the Belgian Congo (one-
third the size of the United States), the jungle had swallowed
them. At the village of Olongombe on the northern bank of the Kasai
they had marked Christmas 1933, and now a two-month trek had
begun. They traveled from village to village on bicycle and on foot,
the smaller children riding on Dad's crossbar. The brothers shared a
bike; one would ride ahead, then lay down the bicycle for the brother
behind to ride while the first walked on. Oh, so much walking.

Nowhere had they seen a store, a clinic, or a building of any sort
other than bark or mud and stick huts. No other white faces were in
evidence. By this time their stock of canned "white man's food" had
dwindled to near nothing. It had been contained, with other supplies, in trunks tied to poles which native porters carried from village
to village on their shoulders. Now the food, more and more, was
native food. This included sour *kwanga*, the villagers' "bread" made
from manioc that had been soaked up to seven days to rid it of the

dangerous prussic acid. It was then steamed, dumped out on a reed tray, and pounded with a pestle to make a large, heavy, sticky lump of a loaf. Monkey, antelope, birds, insects, tropical fruit as available... whatever the people ate was their fare.

Nowhere in the villages had they seen the slightest evidence of what is elsewhere called "civilization"—just heat, hills, swamps, insects, hunger, and disease. They were, after all, on their mission field in 1934. The unvarnished heathen they met were seeing a white woman and children for the first time. The lifestyle and conditions they found among the people had been just as true in 1833—or even further back—as they were in 1933. These were people untouched by anything but the turning of the earth upon its axis in orbit. The passing of hours, days, weeks, months, and years left them as they had been: the same. The same darkness, the same death, the same dearth of the knowledge of the Gospel that had doomed their ancestors to a Christless eternity: all this remained unchanged. This was the mission field of H. E. Grings and his family; a life unimaginable to today's readers.

The weeks passed. Again and again Daddy Grings went ahead to check out the next village, then returned for his family. They had stopped briefly at the government territorial post of Oshwe, and now, a month's journey from Oshwe, they were approaching their goal: the village of Mbongo. It lay a thousand miles into the interior from the sea coast—far north, near the dark waters of the Lokoro River. Once again, Daddy Grings went first to meet with authorities in the village and let them know of the coming of his family, just as a government agent would send a *planton* (messenger) to tell a village of his impending arrival.

The strange little procession arrived in the village, dressed in the garb of the 1930s missionary: a cork helmet on each head and a strip of covered red flannel hanging over their spines outside their clothing (thought at that time to protect from the sun's ultraviolet rays). The expected accommodation would be the usual government rest house, consisting of three rooms made of mud and stick walls and dirt floors. The living/dining/everything room in the center was open in both front and back, with one room on each side serving as a bedroom or storage room.

'To be forewarned is to be forearmed' became a literal truth. They were quickly surrounded by men clad only in their raffia loin cloth, with spears and bows and arrows raised.

"Why are you here?" they wanted to know.

What could this mean? "Do they think we are some of those disliked Belgians? Do they see us as a Belgian family coming to live in their village, making work demands an everyday thing?" the Grings wondered. Didn't they understand the explanation given the other day when the white visitor had told them that he would be back with his family to come stay with them and teach them? Peeking out from behind her mother's skirts, little Louise didn't feel very well protected. But then Daddy Grings spoke, his words a strange, God-given question.

"Do you know God?"

Stunned, the men looked at him in silent disbelief. What a foolish question—"Do you know God?"

"Of course we know God!" was their rejoinder.

"What do you call him?" questioned Daddy Grings again.

"We call Him *Mbombianda*," they replied, "Because He is the Potter who took clay and made us."

"Oh, you do indeed know God," marveled Daddy Grings. "Did you know He has a Son who came to earth to show us the path to His village?"

"No," they replied, a bit bewildered.

"Well," said Daddy Grings, "that is the reason we came here, to tell you about the Son of God. We are God's *planton*, bringing you word from *Mbombianda*."

The spears and bows and arrows were lowered. We were allowed to stay. They were going to hear about the Son of *Mbombianda* and what He came to earth to do. And hear they did—for the next thirteen years.

That message was revolutionary and brought many a one sitting in darkness and the fearful shadow of death into blessed light and eternal life in Christ. It took time, persistence, and patience to pierce through the ancient, entrenched animistic customs and practices. But oh! What joy shone from their faces when they realized that they were free from all the binding fetters of the past. The powerful Word of God broke down the barriers of superstition and false beliefs and brought hundreds to the transformation of "a new creature: old things [being] passed away..." (II Corinthians 5:17). They burned their fetishes, destroyed their idol altars, and the witchdoctors disappeared. It continues today in the twenty-first century to the glory of God.

Incredible as it may seem to some, what you have just read has occurred in many lands down through the centuries. In 1817, the time of Adoniram Judson, the Karen tribesmen in Burma called God *Ywa*. They refused to convert to Buddhism, the state religion, because they considered that to be idolatry. Years passed as they waited for someone to come with The Book which their prophets prophesied would tell them what *Ywa*, the creator God of the universe, had done to save them from their sin. Thousands were saved when Adoniram Judson translated The Book, the Bible.

To the Mbaka people, Bantu of central Africa, He was *Koro*, who had promised to send messengers with His story. One of their villages, Yablangaba, had preserved that wonderful lore and was quick to come to Christ when missionaries arrived in the 1940s. Recently in the year 2000, the Karen tribesmen were mentioned in news around the world, where they were well known to be Christians though living in a Buddhist country.

"Do you know God?" A question asked by missionaries in remote areas, has been answered "Of course we know God," by people lost in their sin but still possessing knowledge somehow filtered through the darkness of their lives by a merciful God preparing them to respond to the Gospel when it arrives. *Mbombianda*, the Potter who took clay and molded us.

"And the Lord God formed man of the dust of the ground, and breathed into his nostrils the breath of life." (Genesis 2:7)

FRUITFUL FIRST TERM

June, 1954.

"It can't be!" I thought as I drove the unfamiliar and challenging streets of Brooklyn. Louise expecting—on our way to Congo? Another child to be born just twenty-two months after little David, our first? How will she handle the ocean trip, sixteen days on a low-slung freighter crossing a sometimes tumultuous Atlantic Ocean? The *Lindi* was a Victory ship, so called because it was mass produced by the Kaiser Corporation to strengthen and rally our merchant fleet for victory during World War II. Victory ships had been designed to sit low on the ocean surface, so as to be less visible to the German U-boats who were turning the Atlantic into a graveyard for Allied ships.

This small freighter was just the beginning of our adventurous first term on the mission field. Our party was made up of my wife Louise, her youngest brother Mark Grings, our little eighteen-month-old son David, and myself. The passenger list was completed by another missionary couple heading back to the Belgian Congo under a different mission. On June 5th we loosed the docking ropes, and with a hoarse sounding of the ship's horn we swung out into the channel.

Two things soon became evident. Firstly, David needed a doggy harness lengthened with rope for additional walking room to keep him from going overboard. The freighter was not designed to carry little children as passengers, and David could easily have fallen through the railing.

The second thing I learned was that waves could come over the side of the ship onto the freight deck. This being my first time on the ocean, the sight of big waves rushing to explode against the bow of the ship *had* to be captured on film. So I found myself down on the freight deck leaning over the rail to catch "one of the big ones"! Which I did—never had so much heavy, salty water poured over me with such force. The picture would have been dramatic if the salt water had not destroyed the camera and the film. On the bright side, Louise had her birthday on June 12, and we celebrated our 3rd wedding anniversary on the 18th, both—rather romantically—on shipboard.

Sixteen days after sailing past the Statue of Liberty and out into the Atlantic, we arrived at the seaport of Matadi on the Congo River. Matadi is about one hundred miles up the Congo River, and to reach it a ship must be capable of at least thirteen knots because of the swift current of the world's second largest river[1]. From there, we drove two hundred hot, hilly, winding miles to Léopoldville[2] , the capital of Congo. We were glad to find lodging in a missionary guest house there. From Léopoldville, a DC-3 flight to Kikwit saved Louise the next lap of the journey; hundreds of rigorous miles over one lane dirt roads and multiple river crossings by either cable or motor ferries lay ahead of us. At some of the rivers, long lines of big freight trucks were ahead of us; at others, the workmen had quit for the day. The

---

1 Second largest in discharge, the Amazon River being the largest.
2 Formerly Léopoldville; also referred to by its current name, Kinshasa, in this book.

ferries were boarded by lifting thick, heavy planks onto them, aligning the wheels of the vehicle with the planks, and cautiously steering onto the ferry. Disembarking on the other side was a repetition of the same process. Over the years some of my shirts, worn thin, were split up the back helping hoist those planks when extra help was needed.

Finally, we crossed our last ferry at Brabanta on the Kasai River thirty kilometers from what we would call home for the next six years, our "jungle rats' nest" at Nkole Nkema. Admittedly, living in a mud and stick house with dirt floors and a thatch roof was not much like the home of my upbringing in Salt Lake City, Utah. But there were more important things to think about, such as learning the Lingala language. Fortunately, Louise and her sister Bessie grew up in the Belgian Congo and spoke the languages fluently. Having had no exposure to language learning, I was now faced with learning Lingala by my own system, which consisted of matching lists of vocabulary words in Lingala with English, and hounding Louise and Bessie for definitions.

About three months later when October rolled around, I was able to survive in understanding and making myself understood. This was just in time for us to make the "birth trip" to the mission station of Kifwanzondo, ten hours away. There we would be close enough to the town of Idiofa for Louise to get help with the birth at a government clinic. Surprises awaited us.

By the providence of God, we were staying on the mission station of Angus and Emma Brower, old time friends and coworkers of the Grings family. The idea was to take Louise about twenty miles to Idiofa in our Chevrolet Carryall[3] when the time came.

---

3   Early variant of the Suburban.

The time came unexpectedly early. I immediately went to the Brower's house to get our car, while Emma quickly went to help Louise get ready. Instead, Emma found her lying on the floor with the birth already in process.

By the time I returned, with God's help Emma[4] had delivered the baby but was dealing with the cord wrapped around his neck. She removed the cord, but he was blue and not breathing well. The usual pat on the seat or flip on the feet did not do the trick. A pan of warm water and one of cold enabled us to warm him and then immerse him in the cold water, which rewarded us with a lusty gasp and cry each time we repeated this process. When at last he was breathing more normally, it was time to load the Chevy and head for Idiofa for some repair work on Louise and a checkup for Baby Jonathan.

Exactly three years later on October 26, 1957, his sister Deborah Louise was born. We went to the Lever Brothers Company clinic in Brabanta on the Kasai River for her birth. We were now a happy family of five: Darrell (myself) and Louise Champlin, with David (5), Jonathan (3), and Deborah freshly minted, living in the deep jungles of Congo with God's good hand upon us.

After six years it was furlough time; we were worn and weary, but enjoying much fruit. Ten congregations were worshipping the Lord and seven schools were making an impact on the darkness of mental and spiritual illiteracy. More than a score of men were studying God's Word in preparation for service. A price had been paid in heat stroke, dysentery, fungi, and parasites which had wasted our bodies. Jonathan had suffered a long bout with hepatitis, but was feeling chipper

---

4   Thank the Lord that years ago, Anton and Viola Anderson and their family had worked with the Grings family in those early pioneer days. A single young man, Angus Brower, had also been serving at the time, and he had married the Anderson's oldest daughter, Emma. It was she who now came to our assistance. The Lord knew, of course, that her help would be needed years later with the delivery of Jonathan Mark Champlin, as related here.

again. We had lived on $28 a month for personal needs.[5] Back in the USA, my mother cried when she saw the wear those six years had made on our bodies.

One of the events that took place during our eighteen month furlough was joining Independent Faith Mission, a fundamental Baptist mission board based out of New Castle, Pennsylvania. We raised additional support for the ministry in Congo, newly christened the Republic of Congo after gaining their independence.[6]

It was time now to return home to Africa. Again we found one of the Liberty ships which offered cheap fare across the Atlantic, sailing this time on the *Vinkt*. We had a little excitement when the ship lost power as the result of a storm. For three days we drifted while the crew replaced the water seal on the main propeller shaft which had been damaged by the storm. Then a bank of clouds, hanging low over a distant mass upon the sea's horizon, announced that we were approaching Africa. The next day we sailed up the Congo River and stepped ashore at Matadi on January 26, 1962. Little did we know at that moment that 1964 would see the disruption of everything we were there to do.

Into the interior we went, now on roads far more familiar than we had faced eight years earlier in 1954. With the series of stops and river crossings (on the same ferries) behind us, we were back on the bank of the Kasai River at Brabanta, now called Mapangu by the new government. Gazing across at our home territory as we ferried over in our new Jeep station wagon, it felt as if we had never been away. Our people, however, felt that we had been away too long—which we were about to find out.

---

5 See the story "No Money, No Work, No School", pg. 203, for further details of our living circumstances during this period.
6 See "Independence: Congo Style", pg. 209

The rutted dirt road, already showing the lack of maintenance by the new government, wound upward from the river through the village of Malembe, mud and stick huts sprawling over the hillside. In the forest we ran into mud in some places, deep sand in others. At last, we broke out into the plain. Many washed-out places faced us as no drain-offs were kept in repair. We made our way around them and jolted through the plain, stopping to greet the Christians in villages along the way.

It was dark as we approached the little valley into which the road dipped just before arriving at our station. Our headlights had been visible for some time already to our Christian village. No message had preceded us, but that did not keep the magic telegraph of human voices from broadcasting the obvious. Those lights at this time of night—it could be none other than their missionaries' vehicle!

So it was that when we arrived at our station, we were soon enveloped by an excited, clamoring crowd. The doors swung open, and we were swarmed with shouting men, women, boys, and girls. Grabbing our hands and pumping them up and down they cried, "*Mbote, mbote, mbote!* (Hello, hello, hello!)" For the next hour there was no way we could leave the spot, till the babble of voices and gesticulations of joy began to subside. Our hands were wrung by hard, hilariously happy grips, and then helped as we carried our luggage into the house. We were home!

A day or two later we got our next surprise. A believer from a hundred fifty miles away at the far end of our ministry to the north presented himself at our door. He had hitched a ride on a truck.

"Where in the world did you come from," I asked, "and why?"

"I was sent by the Christians at Dika, Watu, and Bongemba to tell you how happy they are that you have returned," was his reply.

Then from the eastern end of our ministry came another brother in Christ. He too had come on foot for the believers in Ntombalongo, Ongo, and Mpombi, to express gratitude to God for our return. Brothers and sisters in Christ, we were all grateful to be together again. What a welcome!

The apostle Paul must have felt something of this when he wrote, "Your rejoicing may be more abundant in Jesus Christ for me by my coming to you again." It was for their "furtherance and joy of faith... that [they might] stand fast in one spirit, with one mind striving together for the faith of the Gospel." (Philippians 1:25–27)

JUST JUNGLE RATS

Bordered by the great Kasai River along much of its southern boundary, the Sankuru River on the southeast, and the Lukenie River on the north, the Boldi area where we settled was dominated by a thick rain forest of towering trees and tangled vines. Here and there were scattered patches of grassland called *lisobi* in contrast to what they called the *jamba*.

This was a lush land. Wildlife was abundant; the trees teemed with a plethora of monkeys and birds. *Ngila* were there, the least intelligent of the monkeys. They signaled their presence by calling "mah-ah-nko, mah-ah-nko" while recklessly swinging about in the tall trees. They were ready victims for the poisoned arrows or muzzle loaders of the jungle people. *Nshodji* and *ngei,* two types of spider monkeys, were much more difficult to hunt. The *ngila* troops were indeed fortunate to have the *nshodji* or *ngei* to act as sentries. The *nkolongo* monkeys, large and red, were often discovered through their atrocious smell.

Above and around the monkeys swarmed birds of many sorts, the largest of them being the hornbill. King of the hornbill family was the *mpwa*. Black with broad wings and a huge bill, *mpwa* nested in tree holes high up in the forest canopy. Their approach was signaled long before their arrival by the powerful thrust of their wings. The *jata*, on the other hand, made their black and white coming evident by a loud call. *Bakongo*, their little cousins, were of the same coloring but half the size of a *jata*. The great *eke*, a black and white eagle, sat in the tallest trees and swooped down on its prey, which included fish. Other smaller birds, too numerous to mention here, filled the air with constant movement and sound.

Snakes too prowled the trees. Some caught and ate birds or their eggs. Others, such as the cobra and the deadly green mamba, captured small mammals to make up their diet. Great boas piloted their twenty-foot lengths through the trees and across the ground to seek their prey. To swallow a hundred-pound antelope with six-inch spike horns was a slow, time-consuming process; their dinner would take at least a couple of weeks to digest and create a noisome halitosis![1]

On the jungle carpet also dwelt a number of different species: antelope, wild boar, and rodents of many sizes, shapes and colors. Leopard and several other kinds of cats prowled. The civet cat, or *ja* as the people called him, was a little creature with feet like a dog, a face like a cat, and a body covered with black fur and white flecks. He smelled something like a skunk—fortunately, not too strongly. He spent his nights searching for ground nesting birds and succulent pineapples, or stealing roosting chickens from some unwary perch Elephants traveled trails made both by themselves and humans, feeding on jungle fare and in the gardens of the Bankutu people.

Wild ducks, herons, storks, kingfishers, and other water birds flew up and down the rivers, nesting on the banks or in the swamplands. The ducks in particular liked to feast upon the manioc roots

---

1   Offensively bad breath

that the Bankutu people soaked to leach out poisonous prussic acid before using it as food. Some ducks paid with their lives for this thievery when hunters lay in wait for their early morning or late evening arrival. Five-foot-tall termite mounds in the plains were a common sight, and were sometimes inhabited by a large python after being dug out by a giant anteater who feasted upon the termites. The anteater would dig till he found a ball perforated by many holes through which the drones fed the queen and carried out thousands of eggs. The anteater would find the queen's chamber, enjoy the thumb-sized delicacy for which he had come, the mound would then die, and the termites would swarm to create a new queen and build a new mound.

The plains were also home to numerous other birds and animals. Chief of the antelope was the great bush buck, called *nkai* by the people. Tall and majestic, he wore a beautiful orange-brown coat marked with white stripes and spots and a pair of foot-long spiral horns. The *nkai,* when startled, would bark like a dog. More numerous were the smaller *nse*, which were about the size of a goat. Powerful Cape buffalo feasted on lush grass early and late in the day, and retired to the groves for safety at night. Birds such as guinea fowl, partridges, quail, bustards, and doves were everywhere. When the people burned off the head-high grass of the plains, the great black and white *mpulunjali* herons would gather from their river habitations to feast upon the grasshoppers and other insects fleeing the fires.

The people gathered in villages of small bark and stick huts with palm leaf thatch or grass roofed houses that would fit in many an American bedroom. With little clothing and even less money they eked out a subsistence living from their hunting, fishing, and cassava or rice fields. Their churches were built of the same materials. Harassed by many tropical diseases including malaria, intestinal and skin

29

parasites, hepatitis, fungi, boils, skin ulcers, and blinding eye infections, they lived as had their ancestors: a hand-to-mouth existence.

If asked to describe our experiences as missionaries in the jungles of Congo and Suriname, the designation that applies most aptly would be simply "jungle rats". As of the writing of this chapter[2], we have worked for the past forty-six years with people groups whose circumstances are in many ways a hundred or more years removed from the advanced civilization of the USA. Some would call these folks backward, primitive, or under-developed. But perhaps the most accurate way to project a clear picture of their lifestyle is to describe them as mentally, philosophically, and physically "living in the past". The basic drive of the tribal peoples of African origin is to repeat the past. Our people in Suriname were brought as slaves from Africa in the 1600s and are still dedicated to the preservation of the ways of their African forefathers. In fact, they have been described by anthropologists writing for the Smithsonian Institute magazine as having done a better job of preserving Africa in the jungles of Suriname than the Africans still living in Africa. Their languages are complicated but have a far smaller vocabulary than those of the Germanic, Romance, or Asian languages, and thus they lack the words needed to express modern life as experienced in other areas of the world. They are indeed, internally and in many ways externally, a century or more removed from what the rest of the world calls "today." As a result, they constantly misinterpret the news coming to them from the "outside world". To live with them as a missionary is to physically and mentally step backward in time; to become, in effect, jungle rats.

When we arrived in the Belgian Congo in June of 1954, we were—to be plain about it—blissfully broke. What babes in the woods we

---

2   As mentioned in the introduction, these stories were written during or around the year 2000.

were! Mark Grings, Louise, and myself had trekked across the USA from Los Angeles to Brooklyn, as innocent as could be imagined. Mark and Louise had grown up in Congo as the children of missionary parents, so they were returning to familiar circumstances. Baby David, just over a year old, and I, his father, were on a journey into the unknown. For all of us, traveling across country as missionaries on deputation was an unprecedented adventure. We had scheduled very few meetings and had little money. The result was that our meetings went well in the familiar territory of California, Nevada, and Utah, where our last stop was my home church, Bethel Baptist Church in Salt Lake City. From there on, however, we were truly pilgrims in a foreign land. February, the dead of winter, found us on Route 30, the Lincoln Highway (there were no interstate highways then) in Cheyenne, Wyoming. We had six dollars, a loaf of bread, and a piece of cheese, and we needed to find a place to sleep out of the icy cold.

A rustic, cabin-style motel appeared in the headlights of our borrowed car, and I pulled in.

"Six dollars a night," was the proprietor's response to my query of "How much?"

So I spread our bankroll on the counter, including change, and we became officially broke. This meant that Mark would sleep in the car, since the cabin had only a double bed and crib, just enough for a twenty-two-year-old father, his bride, and little son. But God takes care of His children, and so it came to pass that the owner of the motel, doing his rounds later, came upon Mark in the car and gave us a second room for free.

Thus it was that we crossed the country living from God's hand to our mouth. We didn't dream that there was any other way of doing it. We slept in an unfurnished old farmhouse in Joplin, Missouri, and

31

ended up working for our room and board at East 35th and Avenue J just off Flatbush Avenue in Brooklyn. For three months Louise worked as a domestic, and Mark and I mowed lawns, trimmed trees, washed cars, and painted buildings for the Bible Christian Union in exchange for lodging and meals. Then our visas were granted in spite of the fact that we had been told it was impossible for three nobodies to get visas from the Belgian Colonial government without some kind of on-site official representation. God kept us in Brooklyn for three months in order to give us two more supporting churches and new friends who are still a tremendous blessing to us. This stay raised Louise's and my monthly support level to $168.

So it was that we sailed, armed with faith and insufficient monthly support. The entirety of our earthly possessions rode in barrels and boxes in the hold of the *Lindi*, including a Chevrolet Carryall, a gift from our mission board. At last after fifteen days on the high seas the dark outline of the African continent, brooded over by piles of dark clouds, appeared on the horizon. On the sixteenth day we entered the mouth of the great Congo River, the second largest river in the world, and fought our way upriver against the powerful current until we reached Matadi, a port hewn by the Belgians out of the rocky shore. In fact, the building of this harbor out of the boulders was the origin of the widely held name for white men in Congo, *Mbula Matadi*, "the breakers of rock."

Imagine our surprise when the Belgian customs officials informed us that we owed them $500 in customs fees. Oh my! At the moment, we were still in our usual state of pennilessness. But God—through very helpful fellow missionary passengers—provided a loan of the $500 needed to get our vehicle off the dock. We wired our mission for a loan with which to repay them and went merrily on our way.

Loading our Carryall and a hired truck, we started off for Léopoldville, the capital. We flew Louise on a DC-3 from Léopoldville to Kikwit, as the road was extremely rough and the trip too arduous for a young wife expecting our second son, Jonathan. Mark and I took turns driving on the twisting one lane road, crossing rivers again and again on primitive ferries. This involved lifting thick planks onto the ferry, driving the car onto this makeshift ramp to board, dropping the planks back onto shore, loosing the ferry to be swept back across the river by the current as it tugged against a pulley sliding on a thick cable tied across the water, and then debarking. Picking Louise up at Kikwit and stopping once or twice to see missionaries along the way, we crossed another three rivers and at last stood on the bank of the great Kasai River. Two miles across that broad crocodile and hippo populated river lay our field, eight hundred miles into the interior from where we had landed at Matadi.

And so it was that an hour or two later we pulled up, weary and road worn, in front of a big, rectangular mud and stick house with a high thatched roof. We were home. The house was built of poles cut in the forest, sharpened on one end and driven into the ground forming the outline of the floor plan. Reeds were then tied on both sides of the poles with the tough outer skin of a jungle vine called *nkodi*. The house was literally tied together with vines. Chunks of mud were then stuffed between the reeds, filling the pole frame from top to bottom. Long poles across the top secured the walls in place. The pole rafters were constructed on top of the walls, and wide raffia palm leaf thatch was tied to the frame, again with "jungle nails," the *nkodi* vine. Rough-sawn hardwood boards were nailed into place as window and door frames. The house was plastered with the same mud which had filled the walls, and a clay floor was tamped into place. A clay veranda was filled in between a row of stakes driven into the ground and the outer walls of the house to form a walkway under the overhang of the thick thatch roof. Voilà, our dwelling! Now white and red clay was brought from our hardware store (the jungle), mixed with water in proper proportions, and painted on the walls. We used white from top to bottom and red as a border about two feet high around the bottom of the walls. Inside, reed mats woven by local women covered the clay floor and served as a roof for the millions of termites that protested against our walking on their ceiling by knocking their heads against the mats.

You must understand that a termite colony is made up of several different ranks. The queen is, of course, the most important; she lies in state in a ball of clay with many holes leading down into her room. Fed by special drones, she produces hundreds of eggs each day. Some workers carry the eggs to their incubators, while others act as engineers, building the tunnels that the termites use when they are exposed to the sun, for sunlight kills them. You might say that termites love darkness rather than light because their deeds are evil. Still other termites are soldiers with large orange, flat heads and pincers, and it was those pincers we would hear as we trod on their "roof".

The house had free-standing closets for our clothing, but we had to be careful not to let anything touch the mud walls, or the next morning the termites would have eaten a sleeve off a shirt or some such damage. Shoes left on the floor for a couple of days unworn would be covered with clay by the termites while they worked in the darkness to eat the shoes. In spite of our best efforts to isolate our storage containers from the termites by standing them on smooth metal cans, we were dismayed months later to find that they had invaded the suitcase containing our children's "grow-into" clothing and had turned them into powder.

We used kerosene lamps to light the house. We had a pressure lamp and an Aladdin lamp with its tall slim chimney, rounded base containing the kerosene fuel, and a bright burning mantle. When placed on a table, this lamp made a bright circle of light in the room, but under the table and outside the ring darkness reigned. Since the house had no windows or doors that could be shut, just holes in the wall, it was possible for *anything* to be in the house at any time. In fact, two snakes came and went regularly. We looked them over pretty well and decided they were non-poisonous and more dangerous to the mice, rats, cockroaches, centipedes, tarantulas, and scorpions that frequented the house than they were to us, so we let them live. That seemed the logical thing to do. We did kill poisonous snakes in the house, and once a ten-foot viper in the kitchen house. Louise took care of a snake she once found in her pots and pans cupboard.

That first night we arrived from the USA and lit that Aladdin lamp with its circle of light, Louise's motherly heart wondered "How in the world am I going to let my infant son down on these floors? And how is he going to sleep safely?" The two solutions were, of course, to have faith in God and have common sense—in that order. Faith in God: an ever wakeful, omnipotent, omniscience, omnipresent God Who was competent to watch over our children. Any other thought was both unthinkable and untenable.

The second solution was common sense. The way for our children to be safe at night in a house where anything could and did walk in was to build box beds. We made wooden beds with legs standing several feet above the floor, a board bottom on which the mattresses lay, a screened area, and a wooden roof on which things could be stored. When our children went to bed, beginning with little David, they were safe inside a screened box with a door that was latched from the outside. If they needed to go to the potty (the toilet was a pit latrine outhouse, which we called the reading room) they would call for us, and with a flashlight we would see that they were cared for. And thus we raised three children, bringing all into our jungle nest as tiny infants. And God was faithful—naturally! A quaint nest it was for a pair of jungle rats and their little ratlets.

ON COMING
OUT OF DARKNESS

*"Now when Jesus had heard that John
was cast into prison, he departed into
Galilee; And leaving Nazareth, he came and
dwelt in Capernaum, which is upon the sea
coast, in the borders of Zabulon and Nephthalim:
That it might be fulfilled which was spoken by Esaias
the prophet, saying, The land of Zabulon, and the land of
Nephthalim, by the way of the sea, beyond Jordan, Galilee of the
Gentiles; The people which sat in darkness saw great light;
and to them which sat in the region and shadow
of death light is sprung up."*
(Matthew 4:12–16)

The prophet Isaiah, speaking in Isaiah 8:21–22, prophesies that Zabulun and Naphthalim shall be "hardly bestead (oppressed with anxiety) and hungry: they shall fret themselves, and curse their king and their God...And they shall look unto the earth; and behold trouble and darkness, dimness of anguish; and they shall be driven to darkness."

For the word translated as "darkness", the Hebrew of Isaiah 8 and the Greek of Matthew 4 depict a people in a hopeless state of obscurity, blindness, darkness, destruction, ignorance, sorrow, and wickedness. A people who could be defined as benighted; intellectually and morally overtaken by night. *Benighted*...no word could better depict the jungle peoples of the heart of Congo: intellectually and morally overtaken by night.

But then, it happened. The Light of the World came. Just as predicted in Isaiah 9:6–7, "For unto us a child is born, unto us a son is given: and the government shall be upon his shoulder: and his name shall be called Wonderful, Counsellor, The mighty God, The everlasting Father, The Prince of Peace. Of the increase of His government and peace there shall be no end, upon the throne of David, and upon his kingdom, to order it, and to establish it with judgment and with justice from henceforth even for ever. The zeal of the Lord of hosts will perform this."

"The people which sat in darkness saw great light; and to them which sat in the region and shadow of death light is sprung up." (Matthew 4:16)

It is strange to live with a people who virtually never take baths. Their native cloth is woven from the fiber stripped off the fronds of the raffia palm tree. When first woven, it is cream colored. Worn day after day without washing, it grows progressively darker, impregnated by dirt, sweat, body oils, the ocher paints used to smear their bodies, and whatever other substances with which they come in contact. At last the cloth, filthy stiff and worn thin in spots, is discarded for a newly woven piece.

You understand, of course, that many "improvements" accompany the arrival and presence of missionaries. Historically, missionaries were the first to explore the Dark Continent and other mission fields. Following in the footsteps of the missionaries came the merchants;

brave Portuguese, British, Jewish, Arab, Belgian, and French entre-preneurs brought the famous gospel of Coca-Cola and Singer to the primitive peoples of the world. It is amazing, the out-of-the-way places where you would chance upon a Coca-Cola sign or someone using a hand-turned Singer sewing machine.

Missionaries opened the first roads, built the first bridges, launched the first large passenger-carrying boats, cleared the jungle for the first small plane landing strips, and established the first schools and hospitals. The colonial governments followed in the wake of the missionaries and merchants, and brought order as well as the international corporations and country-wide economic systems completely unfamiliar to the tribal peoples who traded by barter. Missionaries trained the first skilled workers, and they continue even today to supply the majority of the carpenters, bricklayers, mechanics, bookkeepers, secretaries, electricians, teachers, and preachers found in third world countries. This is to say nothing of the huge reservoir of literate people resulting from the network of mission schools spread across Africa. Only recently have some African governments been able to take responsibility for nationwide public schooling. So import-ant are the missionaries to some nations that President Mobutu of Congo once made an appeal to the missionaries not to leave in spite of the horrible conditions in the country, admitting in his words "that Congo is carried on the shoulders of the missionaries." It is incredible that the President of a nation of forty-five million people should make such a statement, but historically true nevertheless.

So it was that we were privileged to bring great changes to the benighted jungle peoples in the heart of Congo, and see them progress for the glory of God.

How would you respond to the presence of missionaries if, for instance, you had never seen a dress, underwear, shoes, a toilet, a kerosene lantern, an electric light, a flashlight, a battery, a washing machine, or an automobile? What would you do with your baby if you had never seen diapers? We have fond and hilarious memories of times when these items were introduced at Nkole Nkema, our jungle station. Allow me to relate a few of them to you.

Our church building at Nkole Nkema was built of tamped clay. That is, I made plywood forms which could be clamped together a foot wide, into which we dumped fresh yellow clay from a pit dug nearby. The clay was then tamped down by rods with a flat piece of board on the end. Once the form was completely full, we scraped it flat across the top with a machete. Releasing the form, we would repeat this process all around the building on top of the tamped clay foundation. By using forms of two different lengths, we were able to leave spaces for windows and doors. Once the clay walls were dried solid, we built a roof frame using poles cut in the jungle and tied with the *nkodi* vine (their answer to nails—and an effective one, at that.) On top of the rafters, thatch from the raffia palm tree was tied. The palm fronds were bent over reeds and sewn together with—you guessed it—the *nkodi* vine. It was about the thickness of a finger, and was first split lengthwise in four sections with the interior fiber stripped off, leaving the pliant, tough skin of the vine. A well done roof of palm leaf thatch would last about five years before so much of the length of the overlap was rotted away that the rain began to find its way through the cracks.

The floor of the church was dirt, of course. The pews were made of split logs laid between forked uprights. An "upholstered pew" would have been a log with its bark still on. The windows were squares between the tamped clay columns that supported the roof frame.

Nothing but air occupied the window space. The door, likewise, was just an opening between the walls at the front of the church.

Young mothers attended the services with their naked babies, who would require attention in two areas during the service. First came hunger, which they loudly announced; no problem, for mother's nourishment was readily available. No shawl covered the mother's shoulder as an American might have; a topless society was the norm and not a head would turn when the mother extended lunch to her eager little one. Diaper service was also unavailable. Baby needs relief? A simple swing out over the center aisle or between the pews allowed for that on the dirt floor, and soft leaves were on hand to use as baby wipes.

On occasion, caring folks back in the USA sent us boxes of used clothing, which stirred great excitement among our national folks. To understand part of the excitement, you must realize the degree of their poverty as compared to the wealth of the average American family—even those on welfare. Jackets were especially desirable to the men, and we often wondered how they could endure them when the temperatures were hovering around 100°F and we were pouring sweat. A used jacket, raffia loincloth, used shoes (likely too large!) and old sunglasses...now *there* was an outfit in which to come to church!

The women were equally taken with feminine clothing. Having never seen underwear, of course they had no idea how to distinguish between men's and women's. Slips passed for dresses, and we frequently answered such questions as "Where is the front or back?" or "Which is inside or out?" Before we caught on, we did not realize how much explanation was needed. It came home to us one Sunday morning when one of the young ladies, feeling very well dressed, walked through the front door of the church with nothing on but her slip! After all, it was a lot more than she had ever worn at one time before.

It became evident that we needed a tailor who could supply the clothing that was becoming increasingly important for the growing congregation of believers. And what about washing the clothing? Now that was a new idea!

When you begin to understand these circumstances, you catch on to the reason most jungle stations often included a little missionary store. They might purchase bolts of cloth to meet the need for clothing, a demand that makes good Biblical sense to the missionary. A type of unbleached cotton cloth as well as a sturdy dark blue material were usually available from Portuguese merchants who made periodic trips to the villages. Long bars of old-fashioned lye soap mixed with bluing and packed in wooden crates could also be purchased. But who would sew these blouses, skirts, shirts, and pants? Louise couldn't keep up with the work. Tailors were the obvious answer; let the people buy the cloth and take it to them for the making. Great idea! But who will teach the tailor? You're right; the missionary wife.

How is it that the missionary's house has light at night, while the houses of the villagers are left in darkness with the setting of the sun? The missionaries have kerosene lanterns hanging in their house, or perhaps a pressure lamp. Add two more items to the missionary store: lanterns and kerosene.

The missionaries find that the entire village, including all of the believers, is illiterate. That means New Testaments, Bibles, and songbooks are irrelevant.

"Why don't they go to school?" you ask. The plain truth is that there is no school. Schools, then, become another part of the missionary task which must be addressed as soon as possible. Without them we have an illiterate church, and are in real trouble when it comes to training national leadership. A school is a must.

So now you must build a building using native materials to save money, at least the first time around. Next you find teachers, usually bringing them from another more advanced tribe. This results in tribal conflicts, differences of life style, and other difficulties.

Finally—Hurrah, the school has opened! But where are the girls? Their mothers, you are told, see no reason for a girl to know how to read. After all, she will spend her life having babies, cooking for her husband, planting and harvesting cassava gardens, and trapping fish in the jungle streams. Does a girl need to know how to read for that? Sigh. The few girls who aspire to attend school and manage to reach a class will be called by their mothers on their way to the gardens or fishing. The girl then slips out of the school room when the teacher's back is turned. Perhaps we'll get the next generation of girls?

The boys do alright in class, but sitting quietly is extremely strange and difficult for them. What about the more mature young men who have come to know Christ, the potential leadership for the budding church? They won't fit in well with the little boys in school. How will they learn to read? It takes more involvement and patience. Learning to read with comprehension will take at least two years, and longer still for trained, mature, indigenous leadership to develop in this kind of tribal society.

Here again we butt heads with the mental and moral darkness in which these jungle villagers have lived for so many generations. There's no concept of a future, heaven, or eternity. In fact, not one of the three thousand languages of Africa had a true future tense or a word for "eternal" or "everlasting" until missionaries taught the concept and developed a word that through use was eventually added to the vocabulary. A great void exists where the concept of God was intended to be.

Sexual morality is an unknown quality, and a virgin girl of thirteen a rarity. As in Noah's time, "the wickedness of man was great... every imagination of the thoughts of his heart was only evil continually." (Genesis 6:5) In many ways a lovable people with delightful personalities, they were however deeply scarred by generations of ignorance and darkness. The ability to lie is a practiced skill. Taboos bind the people in superstition, witchcraft haunts them, and the fear of evil spirits affects every facet of their lives. The common threat of a mother upset with her child was "Watch out, the *bekadji* (evil spirits) will get you!" Our hearts go out to a people oppressed with anxiety, misery, ignorance, sorrow, and wickedness. Death parades across the landscape unopposed.

"And they shall look unto the earth; and behold trouble and darkness, dimness of anguish; and they shall be driven to darkness." (Isaiah 8:22)

But God!

"The people which sat in darkness saw great light; and to them which sat in the region and shadow of death light is sprung up." (Matthew 4:16)

The Light of the World is now shining in the darkness; through the Holy Spirit and the preaching of His powerful Word, many have been brought to salvation; of these, some have been called to service. We list a few: Bekanga, Ituku, Njoko, Ilonga, Nsimba, Iyende, Nkoso, Yakobo, Bosange, Basomia, Belanga, Baende, and Bolopo. Trained and equipped, they lead their congregations scattered across an area of three hundred miles. Godly women have taken their Biblical places in Christian homes and churches, and have become candles to their families, friends, and relatives. Mothers bring children into something unknown in the history of their tribes: Christian homes. The light of the Gospel has delivered hundreds from the darkness of sin and superstition, and changed lives glow in numerous villages.

A people have come out of darkness into His glorious light! People who have become in many ways our closest, dearest friends— and it is marvelous to our eyes.

"And they shall look unto the earth; and behold trouble and darkness, dimness of anguish; and they shall be driven to darkness." (Isaiah 8:22)

LULU BEKANGA:
MIRACLE OF A MURDERER

The village of Nkole Nkema lay steaming in tropical African heat a thousand miles deep in the jungle northeast of Léopoldville, capital of the Belgian Congo. Before the missionary lay a long, broad dirt street lined on both sides with bark shacks roofed with thatch. Each was the same: dirt floors, no windows, a single low door made of palm branch sections, and smoke seeping up from a pile of hot embers in the dark interior. The underside of the roof would be jet black with the accumulated carbon of the usual five-year lifespan of these dwellings.

Basenji, the typical African hunting dogs, stared, growled, and lunged with suspicion. Tiny banty chickens scurried helter-skelter in alarm. Goats bleated as they fled. Naked little children, unaware and unashamed of their bareness, peered from behind their raffia palm fiber skirted mothers. Nubile young women, bare from the waist up and thus proudly proclaiming their impending adulthood, gazed in groups intrigued by this visitor. Men, likewise clad only in palm fiber loincloths, strode with male-like boldness toward their visitor.

For the watching missionary, time as he knew it seemed to scroll backwards a century or so to an existence and lifestyle he could in no way have imagined. This isolated place was Nkole Nkema—his new home, his mission field, and his place to preach the Gospel.

Introductions accomplished, he launched into his first Gospel message, only to be startled by a commanding voice crying, "The first person in this village who believes in this Jesus, I personally will bury!"

The village trembled, for they knew he would do it. The voice belonged to a man called Lulu Bekanga, a man whose very name was enough to send chills up your spine. His mother and brother were both witch doctors, and Bekanga had been steeped in witchcraft and Satan worship from his infancy. He was so dyed in evil that he cared not about the pain inflicted on others. Working as a head policeman for a territorial Belgian agent, he had become a plague of brutal law enforcement upon the villages. His bow and spear, notched with the tally of his victims, enforced the awful truth of his ominous threat... *"The first person in this village who believes in this Jesus, I personally will bury."*

But then the grace of God began to work, for the first person to trust in Christ as his God and Savior was Bokelota Antoine, Bekanga's nephew. Culture forbade him to kill a family member. But then, miracle of miracles, the second person to be gloriously saved was Lulu Bekanga himself! God began a work of utter transformation in his life, and at his baptism he asked to take a new name—Paul. So it was that Lulu Bekanga, the feared murderer, became Bekanga Paul, the Apostle of his people.

What a joy it was to teach him how to read and write, study his Bible, and preach the Word of God. How blessed was our service together traveling the jungle trails over an area of about three hundred miles of jungle. We sat around the same campfires, ate the same

48

jungle foods, and fellowshipped together around the Word of God. He taught me so much about his people, their thoughts and their ways.

I'll never forget how we rode our bicycles through the jungles on our way to the village of Ongo and beyond. We made an agreement with our bicycles that they would carry us where they could, and we would carry them where they couldn't carry us. If you saw firsthand the terrain over which we travelled, you would know that we carried them often! One such place was through the Diou, a tributary of the great Kasai River which runs through the heart of Congo. During the rainy season we would often wade waist deep in the waters of the swamp created by its flooding, carrying our bicycles over our heads. Hippos, crocodiles, and snakes were an ever present potential danger; *tsetse* flies, bearers of sleeping sickness, always buzzed about us and feasted again and again on our blood, giving me many skin ulcers.

On one such trip during the dry season, the forty-kilometer trail was wearing my feet sore. Stopping beside the path, I took my shoes off and began bandaging the blisters. Bekanga Paul came over, stood looking down on me, and said with a smile in his voice, "*Mondele, ojali na masini ya malamu mpenja, kasi pneu na yo bajali mabe mingi.*" Which being translated is, "White man, you have a good engine, but your tires are awful." Yes, what a joy it was to travel with him as we brought the life-changing message of salvation.

Alas, then came the great Simba Revolution. The rebels, trained in Communist Eastern Europe, were bent on destroying everything the Belgians and Portuguese had built, overthrowing the newly independent black government of Congo, and bringing in a communist state. The fire of the rebellion swept Congo from the south and west up through the interior, leaving utter wreckage in its wake. It eventually destroyed all of our thirteen churches and seven schools, murdering hundreds of our believers and twenty of the thirty-six men in pastoral training. During this gruesome tirade of hellish fury, they captured Bekanga Paul. He was bound in a torture hold; his back arched like a bow launching an arrow and his wrists tied to his ankles with wet cords. As the ropes began to dry they shrunk and his feet swelled into melons, his hands into grotesque balloons. Standing over him they stomped on him, ripped the hair from his head, and screamed "Bekanga, if you do not deny this Jesus, we will kill you."

His face clouded with agony, he responded, "You may kill me, but I will never deny my Lord Jesus." How could a man love his Lord Jesus with a love like that? Thus spoke a man who had once cried, "The first person in this village to believe in this Jesus, I personally will bury!"

Yes, the man who had been Lulu Bekanga had indeed become Bekanga Paul, the Apostle of his people. By God's grace, Bekanga and the believers with him were able to escape back into the jungle where they lived for several years in hiding. But that is a story for another time.[1] We are reminded of God's call upon the man whom Bekanga chose to be named after in Acts 9 where he's told what God had planned for him: to "bear His name" and also "suffer for Him." (Acts 9:15–16)

---

1   See "Bows and Arrows Against Automatic Weapons", pg. 283, for the completion of this story.

ILONGA PETELO:
BEARER OF THE MANTLE

Ilonga was born in the mid-1940s and rubbed "clean" with sand on a dirt floor in the village of Nkole Nkema. The hut in which he was raised was tiny—seven by eleven feet, the underside of its thatch roof glossy with carbon from the little wood fire that burned day and night on the floor. No clothes closet was needed; his skin served as his only covering, along with the accumulated dirt of going bathless. His parents wore nothing above the waist; below, his father wore a loin cloth and his mother a wraparound cloth. They too bathed only by accident when caught in a heavy rain.

His childhood was a normal one for a jungle boy. His stomach was often enlarged with worms or protein deficiency and his skin was pocked with sores and fungus itch. Lice grazed in his hair, and his toes were scarred from digging out the pea-sized egg sacks of chiggers. There would often be missing toenails. He played little boy's games of hunting, stalking birds and rodents, and shooting reed arrows into a rolling fiber ball. Naturally, he was steeped in the animism of his people, the presence of demons, and the spirits of the dead. He felt the power of the *longomo* (witch doctor), and watched the honor given to the sacred animals, the wild boar and the leopard. Taboos, too, were a part of his life. Certain foods were forbidden to either his family or his tribe, upon pain of sickness or death. He had no idea why anything having to do with eggs or a chicken was forbidden to his mother, or why she could not eat the meat of the big black *ngila*[1] monkey or the husky black *mbende*[2] antelope so often killed in the hunts. But this was so much a natural part of his culture that he never questioned it. Being enculturated into his people at his mother's breast, it was as normal to accept his culture as it was to relish her nourishment. Soon every fiber of his being had been permeated by being a *monkutu*, a member of the Bankutu tribe. Superstition ruled his thinking and evil spirits his actions just as much as fungi, infections, parasites, and dirt ruled his body.

Finally, the day came as a teenager when he could join the village men in the *djita*[3] (hunt) and be sent with them to a certain area of the jungle by the *longomo* as the result of his communication with the spirits. Over their shoulders a number of men carried long nets woven from the fiber of the *nkosa* vine and attached at each end to five-foot-long sharpened stakes. The rest of the men carried their spears and bows and arrows. Reaching the place indicated by the witch doctor, the first "net man" drove one stake into the ground and unreeled the net from his shoulder. Reaching the end, he would drive the second stake. The second man extended his net from the first and so on until a great half-circle of net was formed. Fanning out in a half circle the other men would shout, clang their machetes and spears against trees, and in general make a great ruckus, driving the encircled animals toward the waiting nets and the spears of the net men hiding there.

---

1   Pronounce it through your nose with your tongue against the roof of your mouth: *n-n-n-gila*.
2   Not *mu-bende*, but *m-m-m-bende*
3   In the deep central jungles of Congo, the principal method of hunting is the *djita* (pronounced *gee-tah*).

But sometimes there would be a herd of wild boar in the encirclement. These would stream at great speed toward the nets and follow their leader through the hole ripped by his great sharp tusks. The antelope and other milder beasts would run headlong from the noise into the waiting entrapment of the nets and death. On occasion a leopard would be encircled. Too sharp-eyed to run into the net, he would return toward the noise-making drivers. Pity the man who met the leopard face to face.

Men were maimed or killed in such encounters[4], but here Ilonga gained lasting fame. For he single-handedly withstood a leopard, pinning it to the ground with his spear and defeating its every effort to reach him. Again and again the leopard would claw itself up the shaft of Ilonga's spear, only to be hurled back. So the battle raged until the other men arrived and dispatched this most revered of animals. In triumph, they marched back to the village with their booty, carrying the leopard hanging with his feet down from a pole as if he were marching into the village alive. His body was reverently hung in the place of esteem marked by a plantain tree at the witch doctor's altar. He would eventually be skinned and eaten, but not without a village dance in his honor. The heroic hunter led the dance, prancing in the tasseled skirt reserved for just such occasions. Some of the young men watched and dreamed of the day they might be the one. Others watched hoping their courage would never be so challenged.

Having learned to read in the missionary school, a day came when Ilonga talked with Louise and was wonderfully saved and transformed. He was then perhaps eighteen years old. Trained under Darrell (myself), Ilonga was gifted with discernment and faith beyond his years and his ministry was an extraordinary one from the beginning.

---

4 "Mauled by a Leopard", pg 121

Then came the Simba revolution, the terror of being pursued in the jungle by bloodthirsty soldiers, and finally, Bekanga's dying challenge: "Who will be the Elisha to bear the mantel of departing Elijah?" Ilonga stepped into the gap. His first duty was to direct the burial of the people's Elijah. "We will bury him in the Christian burial ground," was his bold announcement.

"Impossible," cried some of the crowd. "The burial ground is beside the road, in plain sight and earshot of the soldiers."

"I know that," was Ilonga's reply, "but God has shown me the soldiers will neither see nor hear us."

With that, they followed their new leader over the jungle path back toward the very lair of the enemy. As they stepped from the jungle onto the dirt road just a hundred fifty yards from the soldiers' encampment, they could hear the soldiers talking and see them moving about. Some of the believers hung back at the edge of the forest. Others stepped boldly onto the road. Within a few feet of the road they began to dig Bekanga's grave. The soldiers seemed to be entirely unaware of their presence. Seeing God's hand at work, the Christians grew bolder. Soon songs of praise sprang from their lips and triumphant music wafted toward Heaven. Next came testimonies, and a message from God's Word followed. Up the road, the soldiers carried out their functions oblivious to what was taking place just shouting distance away. So it came to pass that the Apostle of his people, Bekanga Paul, was buried while his Lord prepared a table before him in the presence of his enemies. Can you imagine the consternation of the soldiers when they found that fresh grave? Ilonga told me this story while we stood near the ruins of our little house which had been burned by our people in order to deny the soldiers its use.

This was not the only instance in which God displayed His omnipotent sovereignty. On another occasion, Ilonga and his sister-in-law Kampia (Bekanga's wife) were captured by the soldiers. Tying them in a torture hold with their wrists bound to their ankles behind their backs, the gloating soldiers declared their captives would die in the morning. At midnight Kampia was moaning with pain and trembling in anticipation of their death only hours away.

"Don't be afraid, Kampia," encouraged Ilonga. "God has shown me a soldier will come very early and release us." The sky was just beginning to show signs of the coming day when a soldier slipped quietly up, cut their bonds, and whispered *"Run!"* The Psalmist whispered, "Though I walk through the valley of the shadow of death, I will fear no evil: for thou art with me." (Psalm 23:4)

At last, the day came when the soldiers started breaking camp. Having received permission from their president to suspend their failed attempt to annihilate our people, they were preparing for departure. At that moment, into their camp walked Ilonga. Astonished, they watched his approach.

"I have come to take over," he announced.

"Let me kill him!" cried one of the soldiers.

"No, do nothing;" was the commander's reply. "This people and their God have defeated us with bows and arrows, and their leader has the right to take command. Sir, the place is yours."[5]

This people, and their God.

This people and their God-empowered leader, Ilonga Petelo, Bearer of the Mantle. Incredible, but true.

Ilonga Petelo continues to pastor his church in the village of Nkole Nkema deep in the heart of Africa, with the anointing of God

---

5   See "Bows and Arrows Against Automatic Weapons", pg. 283

still evident upon him. God's promise to Joshua is very fitting. "There shall not any man be able to stand before thee all the days of thy life...I will be with thee: I will not fail thee, nor forsake thee. Be strong and of a good courage...the Lord thy God is with thee whithersoever thou goest." (Joshua 1:5–9)

ROGUE ELEPHANT

In the darkness of the jungle just to the east of us a giant beast brooded. He had been wounded in his shoulder when one of those 'little bugs' on two feet had thrown a spear at him; it wasn't much more than a scratch, but it festered. What trouble it had caused him! His ill-temper had forced the herd to put him out, and now he was alone instead of with his kind. But he had shown those two-legged insignificants what for! He had destroyed their gardens and even charged through a whole group of people, sending them running headlong for safety. Everywhere he found a human scent, he wreaked havoc.

One could imagine him relating it, "Like yesterday, when I smelled that hated odor all around a pond of water and the dam which held it, I trampled it—I did! I used it as my toilet. That will show that two-legged 'little bug'! Someday, perhaps, we will meet face to face, that interloper and I. Someday, perhaps—for this is my territory."

Meanwhile, I had found an issue of a *Reader's Digest* condensed book particularly interesting. Especially enticing was a story called "Elephant Jim"; its hero was a professional bounty hunter who had dealt with man-eating lions, leopards, tigers, and rogue elephants in

Africa, India, and Burma. Rogue elephants...that really caught my eye, because of the aforementioned one in our area. He stood ten feet tall at the shoulder with five-foot-long tusks, and he was making shreds of the people's cassava and banana fields.

Ordinarily, elephants are not active in the heat of the day, preferring shady places or water holes. But this fellow had been escorted out of his herd by a couple of big bulls after he had been wounded in the shoulder. One day, he passed near a village several kilometers from us in broad daylight. The men rushed out after him, only to be scattered into headlong flight by the angry animal's wild charge. His next target was the water pool we had created by damming a spring at the hillside where the plain joined the jungle a mile from us. He broke our little dam, trampled everything in sight, and defecated in it.

"So there," he must have thought with satisfaction. "See if you can do anything about it!"

That was the last straw. I determined to meet him face to face before someone was killed by this rampaging beast.

The fateful day dawned with a heavy fog touching the ground. It was dry season, and the Lord was taking care of the antelope of the plain that depend on the wet, dew-laden grass of the dry season mornings for their sustenance. Returning through this thick fog was our mail carrier who had traveled by bicycle the day before to the palm oil plantation about thirty kilometers away and across the Kasai River where we were able to send and receive mail. Suddenly, to his horror this massive elephant materialized out of the thick whiteness. The young man, who came from a tribe unaccustomed to hunting elephants, abandoned his bicycle and ran headlong through the plain, down the hill to our water hole, and up the foot path to our house shouting, "*Ndjoko ejali kuna, ndjoko ejali kuna!* (The elephant is out there!)"

Rising from our breakfast table, I called for Ituku and Ndjoko, two experienced elephant hunters who had regaled me with terrifying tales of their exploits and close escapes. Loading my .30-06 bolt-action rifle with six 220-grain Winchester Silver Tip cartridges, I started out the back of the house.

"Where are you going?" inquired my wife.

"To get that elephant," I responded.

"How many cartridges do you have?" she pursued.

"Six," said I. "Five in the magazine and one in the chamber with the bolt off cock and the safety on. But I only need one, a shot through the temple, as Elephant Jim instructed in the book."

"You had better take more," was her rejoinder. So I stuffed the rest of the box in my back pocket, giving me a total of twenty.

As Ituku, Ndjoko, and I got into the Chevy Carryall, I was reviewing elephant hunting *a la* "Elephant Jim".

"Remember," he wrote, "You cannot penetrate the forehead of an African elephant with ordinary hunting ammunition, the skull being far too thick and constructed like a sponge. Try shooting a charging elephant at the base of the trunk, as the pain may turn his charge. But the shot of choice is the temple where the bone is thinnest." So off we drove on what turned out to be an exciting and dangerous battle that lasted nearly five hours.

We descended the winding, sandy road from our house into a small valley, climbed the other side of the narrow track, and leveled off toward the area where we would find our quarry. There we found droppings in the middle of the road. The fog was lifting and we could see that he had left the scene. Extremely fresh tracks led us toward the jungle looming up several hundred yards through the plain.

Then we spotted him; he stood facing us with his ears spread and his trunk raised in the breeze. Our scent had already warned him of our approach. While an elephant is very near-sighted, his huge ears and keen sense of smell make it difficult to approach him undetected. As we came nearer, he wheeled suddenly and disappeared into the jungle.

Now, elephant trails are formed like a funnel: narrow at the bottom, where they plant each foot in the print of the one ahead, and spreading like a "V" higher up for the passage of their wide bodies. Ordinarily, this enables them to travel silently through the forest. This fellow, however, was making a lot of noise, in effect inviting us to follow. Obviously this was not his first encounter with hunters, and he meant to ambush us.

In order to appreciate the story, you need to understand that an elephant is invisible when standing in mottled sunshine and shade. The light and shadow on his neutral gray skin creates a perfect camouflage, and many a hunter has walked into range of the beast's trunk or tusks without seeing the waiting animal.

Following his trail, I eventually spotted him pulling fruit from a tree on the edge of an old, overgrown cassava field. His head kept bobbing, making it impossible to get a temple shot. Suddenly, he charged us! Ituku and Ndjoko disappeared in a flash, but I, rookie that I was, would have been caught in a few steps had I turned tail. Surely I would have tripped and fallen or been caught in a thicket through which the elephant could easily thrust himself. But in God's providence[1], there at hand was a giant tree formed by a network of

---

1   God's providence, you understand, is a combination of the sovereignty of God and the goodness of God.

roots coming up out of the ground and joining at about ceiling level to create the trunk of the tree. Into those roots I scrambled, crawling to where I was out of reach of his trunk or tusks—a situation which did not please him at all. Screaming and grunting, he worked to get me, trying to lift the tree. All the while I was shouting at him, "If you stick your trunk in here, you will get the hottest nose an elephant ever had." Tiring of the effort, he swung off through the razor grass and thorns of the overgrown field.

Immediately my two erstwhile assistants appeared, and the three of us advanced through the field following the elephant's tracks. Approaching the jungle on the other side of the field, it suddenly dawned on us that the elephant was now where he could see us but we could not see him. He could be waiting for us just inside the jungle. Getting down on our knees, we tried to peer through the tangle as close to the ground as possible, as it is often easier to see *through* the jungle below the maze of leaves and vines that begins higher up.

He was there—four big feet facing us! We had no sooner stood up than he charged. Again, my two erstwhile hunters disappeared. This time, remembering the advice of "Elephant Jim", I raised my rifle, determining to shoot the elephant at the base of his trunk between his eyes the moment he broke out of the jungle's edge. And soon he did! He was now about sixty feet away. *Whack!* Startled, he grunted and wheeled. *Whack! Whack!* My gun spoke twice more in rapid succession, hitting his shoulder as he disappeared back into the tangled forest.

Twice more he laid ambushes for us as the morning wore on, each time choosing a place where he was difficult to spot and facing his tracks on the ready as we moved toward him. Twice more, a shot in that painful area turned his charge, when my gun spoke twice more

61

on the mark. With my little "pea-shooter" of a .30-06 deer rifle, it was like shooting a cow with a BB gun. There was no possibility that a frontal shot was going to stop him. He had to be turned from his charges until I got that temple shot.

Next he led us to what must have looked like the perfect ambush. Here he was going to get us out into the open. A heavy storm had toppled three huge trees rotted at the cores, widening a space that was clear but beginning to fill up with broad bladed leaves. The five-foot-diameter trunks lay in a row, their branches tangled and broken, while just beyond was some mottled sunshine and shade into which the elephant disappeared.

This was the showdown. I reloaded, climbed up on the first trunk and stood waiting, challenging him to come out into the open. Peering into the ring of jungle circling the clearing, I concentrated on catching the slightest movement that would indicate he was there. At last! He's hurting and can't stay still. He's there all right, just yards away and waiting to charge.

"Watch out if he trumpets," Ituku warned. "That sound is so terrifying it will melt your spine. If you don't recover quickly he will be upon you. Others have lost their lives at just such moments."

Here and there echoed the sound of a flight of birds, the call of monkeys gathering to feed, or the buzz of insects. A tree limb broke off and fell, reaching the earth with a thud. All these were the familiar sounds of the jungle. Still the elephant waited.

Then! He trumpeted a shrill, trilling thunder that sounded like a diesel locomotive coming through the jungle. Out of hiding he came—high stepping, ears flared like two flags, his trunk drawn up like an accordion, head bobbing in a great swing up and down.

Crack!

I fired as he came over the first log. He ignored it and crossed the second.

Crack!

Again he shrugged it off. Now he was coming up onto my log. I bounded off backwards; now he was standing over me, head tilted back, his trunk raised like a club to deal the crushing blow. With him towering over me I swung my rifle from the hip and drilled a shot through the roof of his open mouth. With a roar he toppled backwards.

"Ha! I got you!" I shouted. Leaping back onto the log I shot him in the back of the head—

And he stood up.

Now it was my turn to hide! Behind the log I crouched. *"Lord, this gun is too small!"* The elephant swayed as he tried to retain his footing, oblivious of me. I pressed against the log, motionless and holding my breath; he at last began to move. Slowly he picked his way out of the clearing and back into the darkness of the forest. We let him wander on, giving him time to go down.

Minutes later we started after him, but this time without following his tracks. Walking in single file at right angles to where he had gone, we kept careful watch in every direction and noted that his tracks had not crossed the way we were going. Down the slope we found a little stream, clear, without the riling of dirt that would have indicated he had crossed it. Now we knew where he was—to our right and on the slope of the hill. After perhaps a half hour I spotted him across the stream and up the slope, on his knees. A shot through the tangle and darkness roused him, fueling a mighty, defiant bellow of pride and pain. A surge of sadness mixed with the sure knowledge of impending victory coursed through my veins. I quickly crossed the stream and closed the distance as he staggered off. To my astonishment he flattened bushes, walking right over them. Bumping into larger ones, he stumbled back like a drunk might from a street light.

Then he found a good ambuscade and quickly slipped into the disguise and faced his tracks, expecting us to follow. But I was off to the side watching, and now—finally—he stood where I could get my first temple shot.

Crack! It was my last bullet and for a moment he was still upright. But to my great relief, as I looked on, he started dropping slowly and majestically. He did not fall on his side, but straight down; his giant tusks knifed into the ground like a fork, his trunk straight out in front. Slowly, his legs folded under him. Still kingly in death, the battle was over. In his madness, this monarch of the forest had been indeed a very real threat to the lives of the villagers and an initiator of much destruction, but the thrill of victory was still tinged with more than a little sorrow and also great respect. It was noon; the confrontation had lasted almost five hours.

Word spread quickly, and our Christian village folk, as well as those from the heathen village, came with axes, machetes, and baskets. What a sight it was to watch them butcher that elephant! First they used axes to hack off the hind leg section; once it was separated, it was pulled away by a large group of men. Then two men bent over and walked into the rib cavity as they would have entered a small hut. We could hear them talking in there. They brought out the heart, punctured many times by the shots I loosed when I turned the elephant's charges. The gun was indeed too small, for shots through the heart had not stopped him. Many baskets of meat were carried away by all. Smoked over low fires, it provided the people with needed meat for weeks to come.

The government confiscated my gun because I did not have a

license to kill an elephant, but later authorities returned it once they understood the circumstances and the threat of a rogue elephant rampaging through the area. Perhaps a determining factor in the reversal of judgment was also the passionate protests and intercession of the local villagers over the injustice of taking the gun from a man who had risked his life to protect and feed them. The tusks were kept by the government, but the skull adorned our front yard. His monstrous molars, polished and mounted on hardwood, made excellent and striking bookends. It takes a good-sized book to move an elephant molar. As Psalm 46:1 says, we found God "our refuge and strength, a very present help in trouble."

A LEOPARD AT THE WINDOW

The African leopard is not to be toyed with. Known for his strange combination of secretiveness and boldness, as well as his taste for human flesh when once introduced to it, he is formidable to say the least. Ordinarily, it is a wounded leopard that is temporarily hampered in pursuit of his usual wildlife diet who turns to human game. But once he discovers how easy it is to stalk these slow, weak, two-legged creatures who can neither run nor fight, the man-eater may never return to the more difficult task of stalking the swifter, stronger wild game. Such leopards are not common, but have on occasion terrorized African and Asian communities. They have been known to drag their victims from their beds or off their boats in the night, as do tigers in the swamplands of coastal India. Their guttural cough at night is enough to send chills up the strongest back.

In two of these African stories[1], I have mentioned the African leopard, seven feet long including the tail, thirty inches at the shoulder, three hundred steel-coiled pounds as a full grown male. I have met two of them, one in the daytime, the other at night. The daytime

[1] "Ilonga Petelo, Bearer of the Mantle", pg. 51, and "Mauled by a Leopard", pg. 121

fellow was crossing the road in front of me—a beautiful sight which soon disappeared into the tall grass at the roadside. The other came to visit us at night, and he did all the looking.

Rain poured down that day as only tropical rain can. Our mud and stick house was pounded by the winds; the thatch roof yielded here and there and let the rain drip inside. We collected the leaking water in pots and pans rather than let the beds, cupboards, chairs, and tables get wet. The sky cleared at last and the cool evening followed the path of the setting sun as it slid down the hill, across the plains, and finally disappeared behind the dark outline of the jungle. Now indoors and outdoors were one as the night occupied our house. Spiders began to venture forth onto the walls, and in the thatch overhead tarantulas began their eight-footed walk. Mice poked their heads out of their daytime retreats. Bats and night birds flitted. Lo-ou-tas, so named to mimic their lo-ou-ta call, called to each other as they swept by and landed on the path next to our house. (I caught one of them one night by shining a flashlight in its eyes while slipping my hand behind her in the darkness. After taking a good look at her feathered finery I released her, only to find in my hand a beautiful miniature blue egg. Sorry, lady!) Owls began their sharp-eared, swift-winged stalk, and the snakes their heat-sensing hunt. Civet cats rose from their daytime beds and sniffed their way to ground-nesting birds and other delicacies. The monkeys settled down for the night in the safety of their tree homes, though still on guard against snakes and other enemies. Driver ants stirred from their leaf and pelletized earth bivouacs and marched in ground-covering millions to terrorize all in their path. Antelope geared up for another night spent shivering in apprehension. Somewhere, not far away, a leopard coughed.

Our Aladdin lamp glowed on the table, pushing the night back

68

toward the corners of the room. In my tiny office the gasoline pressure lamp hissed its defiance of the darkness and threw shadows on the whitened clay walls. It was working pretty well now; I had used a wood fire to heat its coiled generator until it glowed, then plunged it into cold water, thus breaking up the carbon collected inside so its coil could be removed and cleaned. There was no money to buy a new generator, so ingenuity prevailed, lest darkness should.

It was nearly time for bed. Devotions had been held, and the boys were in their screened box beds, safe now from whatever crept, crawled, slithered, or flew. We made a flashlight trip into the darkness to our pit latrine outside, where at night you could expect to find dark-loving creatures such as scorpions or centipedes on patrol. During the day we jokingly called it "the library" because of old catalogs and other reading material that might be located there.

The mosquito net was next. Louise made our nets with a cotton cloth canopy the size of the bed. The sides were made of netting, while a cotton border bounded the hem to be tucked under the mattress. Even driver ants could be kept outside our bed by this excellent draping.

We used a kerosene lamp to light the bedroom while we prepared to turn in. Our shadows played on the mud-plastered walls as the sounds of the outdoors came clearly through the aperture we called our bedroom window. No screen or glass impeded the flow of cool night air, and the conversations of various night birds, insects, and animals carried on the breeze. My .22 caliber rifle stood in the corner nearest my side of the bed and a flashlight lay beside my pillow.

With a poof we extinguished the little kerosene lantern and tucked ourselves in. Again our house was one with the outdoors in the darkness. Off in the distance a bush baby sang its evening song.

69

Amazing, the vocal strength of that little fist-sized member of the monkey family. The leopard had moved closer to our compound, but no sound betrayed his presence. Other night creatures, though, spotted him and made a hurried retreat.

Sometime in the night he reached the edge of our cleared area. With light gathered from the stars his eyes took in the scene. A U-shaped dirt driveway entered the east end of the lot, turning north off the one lane dirt road that continued its westward journey through the vast jungle and on through grass plains polka-dotted with dark groves. Acacia trees ablaze with yellow flowers bordered the compound at the roadside. Our house stood silently in the darkness a hundred feet back. The driveway curved past the house and turned right; on the bend stood a smaller, grass-roofed guest house. The sweet scent of our pineapple patch perfumed the night air. He paused, glancing at the avocado and papaya trees. The Chevrolet Carryall caused him to stiffen for a moment. But it was inanimate; unthreatening.

His feet padded toward our house. Cautious, every sense on high alert, he moved like the breeze itself. The lo-ou-ta departed. Mice disappeared. Insects stilled. The King was here.

He reached the house. A strange smell assailed his nostrils— sweet, warm. Soft sounds came from inside. A child turned in his screened box bed. Entrance would have been easy. The shuttered windows were no real barrier; a flip of a paw and his head would have been inside. The large open space at the back, twelve feet wide, was our eating area and covered only with a drop reed mat. It could have been easily accessed. He sniffed at the cook house; it was separated from the dwelling by a twelve-foot-long, slightly elevated dirt walkway. Like the main building, it was constructed of mud and sticks with a thatched roof. The smell of smoke reached his nostrils, stronger now that he was near the wood stove standing in the middle of the primitive kitchen.

Exploring, he padded past the unrolled bamboo mat over the back entrance and followed the clay veranda to his right. Four feet wide and about a foot high, with sharpened stakes driven close together to help contain the clay, the veranda circled the house under the protection of the roof's wide overhang. It was wet from the day's driving rain and the cushioned feet of the leopard left their imprint as he moved down the bedroom side of the veranda.

The humans' smell was growing stronger. One of them rolled over and the leopard paused, crouched, tail whipping. Quiet again. His feet glided soundlessly toward the shuttered window, his whiskers twitching as that smell filled his nostrils. Warm, sweet, soft. He stood facing the window, his paws making deep impressions in the soft clay. There, just four feet away, was a strange little net house within which lay two sleeping human beings. Weak creatures, they. An easy meal if he so desired.

But the God of Heaven said "Be gone!" and he said, "Yes, Sir."

And so it was that those weak creatures awoke in the morning, amazed to find the large leopard paw prints outside their bedroom window. They voiced a grateful "Thank you, Lord!" and II Chronicles 16:9 proved true once again:

"The eyes of the Lord run to and fro throughout the whole earth, to shew Himself strong in the behalf of them whose heart is perfect toward Him."

"The angel of the Lord encampeth round about them that fear him, and delivereth them." (Psalm 34:7)

ITUPA,
THE BUZZING SNAKE

"For He shall give His angels charge
over thee to keep thee in all thy ways."
(Psalm 91:11)

Most of our travel on the jungle roads and trails in Congo was accomplished on foot and bicycle. Ituku and I, as well as Bekanga, Ndjoko, Ilonga, Yakobo, Basomia, and others, often made evangelistic trips either to the northwest toward the Lukenie River before then branching off eastward where a string of villages lay scattered throughout the stream-laced jungle, or to the southeast meeting at last the northern bank of the great Kasai River. Either path entailed about a hundred fifty miles of travel. We also reached shorter stretches to the south and southwest.

On one such evangelistic trip, Ituku and I were headed northwest up one of the more rugged roads, riding our bicycles with our saddlebags loaded. Over my shoulder hung my .22 caliber Remington 550-A rifle. Over his was my .30-06, *Makalele Monene* (the Big Noise). On both sides of the road the jungle was dark, as usual. In many places the canopy of two-hundred-foot-tall trees masks the ground so well that direct sunlight has never touched it. In some places a swath several yards wide extended from the edge of the road to the forest.

In other places, particularly in the swampy areas, the jungle closed in and roofed the road.

Hornbills flew overhead, sometimes pausing to eat from roadside trees. Little hornbills like the *bakongo*, and larger black and white *jatas* with double beaks and measuring twenty inches from head to tail, cawed loudly as they circled and called others to a treetop feast. Ituku would vote for going after those, perched a hundred or more feet up, although they were restless and difficult to focus on. Several had already fallen to my .22, however, ensuring something for the pot—either ours, the chief's, or the elders' of the next village at which we stopped. Only rarely did we hear the heaving, whistling beat of the *mpwa*—largest of the hornbills, black as night and extremely wary.

Then...monkeys. Now Ituku's eyes lit up. Here was real meat! A couple of those slung by their tails over his handlebars would be a rich prize indeed.

"*Monsieur, tokenda na bango!* (Sir, let's go to them!)" he said.

So we leaned our bicycles against trees, slipped our gun slings off our shoulders, and melted into the forest. We could hear the monkeys chattering, the swoosh of swinging branches, and the husks of the fruit or nuts upon which they were feeding pattering down like rain to the ground below. Sometimes droppings fell and urine misted down, too. We approached carefully, lest we alert their sentries. But wait! Another sound was here: grunting, moving feet, and tusks digging into soil and ripping at the roots of prized herbs.

Nshombo were there, the big red boars of the forest. Suddenly the stakes in this game were raised and the .22 rifle in my hands was not the weapon of choice. *Makalele Monene*, please! Ituku silently handed me the .30-06 and took the .22 from my hand. We moved forward again, watching every step, eyes above and on the ground at the same time. There must be no sound of warning, no scent drifting to the sharp nostrils of the wild boars. The hunt had become serious.

Then,

Buzzzz.

I froze. Many jungle sounds had echoed in my attentive ears, but never that buzz. Without moving my feet I searched the ground, my eyes straining in the gloom to see the origin of that chilling sound. Then I spotted it: a massive snake some five feet long, its thick body painted with a diamond pattern much like a rattlesnake. Its head was the size of my doubled fist and it stood raised, mouth gaping, body coiled to launch its deadly strike.

Buzzzz, it said again. It was not the sound of a rattle clattering together, for no rattles adorned the tail of this snake. This sound emanated from somewhere within the serpent.

Strange are the thoughts that pass through one's head at such a time. Mine was, "If I shoot this thing with my .30-06, the wild boars will be sure to hear it and run."

I wonder what the snake was thinking. Perhaps, "Why does this two-legged thing not move again? Go on—move! and I will strike you."

"Ituku," I whispered, "Give me my *bonduki moke* (little gun)." Gingerly, his eyes on the fierce something coiled just feet away, he handed me the .22 and took *Makalele Monene.* Slowly, with a minimum of movement, I sighted down the barrel of the .22 and pulled the trigger.

Crack!

The .22 spoke, and the bullet leaped forward and pierced the snake between the eyes. Back it whipped, its muscular body writhing in death. Alas, to our ears came the sounds of monkeys departing at full speed, branches swaying and lifting as the throng made a hasty retreat. But the departures were not confined to the trees; we heard the grunts and squeals of the wild boars, upset at having their breakfast interrupted but more concerned about leaving for other, safer parts.

Oh, well. Ituku severed the head of the *itupa* with his machete and carried the body back to his bicycle. It would make a decent meal, he said, though not as nice as wild boar.

"Missionary," he said as we stood beside our bikes getting ready to move on, "God is with you. The *itupa* only buzzes after he strikes. God must have told him to buzz this time before he struck. Thank God for His goodness."

Yes, thank God for His goodness. "Because he hath set his love upon me, therefore will I deliver him: I will set him on high, because he hath known my name." (Psalm 91:14)

SIXTEEN-FOOT PYTHON

After living in our mud and stick 'jungle rat's nest' for five years, it was evident that the house was so destroyed by termites it would not last much longer. The determined little creatures had literally eaten us out of house and home. That it was time to build a new house was evident, but make it out of what? Build another mud and stick house? How about a tamped clay house with a palm leaf thatch roof? What about using handmade sun-dried bricks? If we put up the thatch roof first on sturdy poles and braced it so the winds would not throw it to the ground, we could build the walls up to meet the roof. In fact, that is the only way to build a brick house during the eight-month rainy season.

Our options were limited by our economic situation, which was, frankly, broke. Our monthly support of $168 was sometimes deposited late, thus unavailable in Congo, and we were giving people IOU's while waiting. Usual donations from our supporting churches were between $5 and $25 a month, and we had virtually no correspondence with the churches. So it was not exactly an auspicious time to consider building a house.

But God knew differently. He laid it on the heart of our home church in Salt Lake City to send us a special $500 gift. Wow! We were rich! We could buy corrugated galvanized roofing and cement to build ourselves a cement block house. So began our block-making project. We would need approximately 2,400 blocks to build a 30' x 30' house with block walls outside and partitions inside. Let's see if those termites can chew on cement! The school children carried sand in buckets from the little stream down in the forest where we took our water. Barrels of water were filled and refilled from the same stream. We labored together mixing cement by hand, tamping the mixture into two metal forms, and turning them over to leave nicely molded cement blocks standing on boards laid on the ground. Working in the dry season, we needed no shelter for the blocks. A rare passing dry season shower would only help our handiwork to cure stronger.

So it happened that one day while we were making blocks, excited women came running up the path from our water hole.

"*Mondele, Mondele, yaka noki. Tomoni mboma ya monene mpenja!* (White man, white man, come quickly. We have seen a python, truly big for sure!)" the women called.

Picking up my ever present .22 caliber rifle, I went down the trail after the women, descending the hill to the jungle. We could smell the snake a fair distance away before seeing it. What a monstrous case of halitosis! Stretched out near the stream, his head raised with a malevolent stare and his body swollen with prey, it was obvious he was there for the purpose of digesting his sumptuous meal.

Evidently the python had laid in ambush near the stream after ascertaining that the inhabitants of the forest came to that spot for a drink, such as various rodents, wild boar, anteaters, and antelope. Spring-tight for launching himself upon his prey, he watched unmoving as the antelope approached. No fool, it paused again and again as it neared the water. Head up, tail switching, looking from side to side, it tried to decide if it was safe enough. The snake, however, was well hidden and motionless. His skin had been designed to blend perfectly with the dappled forest floor. Sunlight straggling through the overhead canopy of trees, vines, and saplings was scattered randomly here and there, perfecting the camouflage. The enemy was invisible and patient. At last, the antelope stepped in and lowered its head to lap the sweet, cool water. The python's strike was swift, silent, and sure.

Stricken, the antelope staggered back, the great snake's long, fishbone-like fangs gripping its shoulder. Thick heavy coils wrapped around the antelope as it struggled to rise and flee. The snake's tail, equipped with a hard, horny point, dug into the earth behind a root. Anchored, the snake contracted his muscular body and the antelope's bones began to snap.

The brief battle over, the crushed antelope was swallowed head first, the jaws of the python unhinging to allow his mouth to engulf his prey. With his stomach bulging, the python maneuvered into a comfortable position near enough to the stream to take an occasional drink and began his lengthy digestion. It was then that the women smelled him.

Staring at me he hissed, open-mouthed. My rifle spoke, and he fell back, folding and unfolding over himself. Then he was still. The workmen with me cut a stout pole and gathered some of the strong, finger-thick *nkodi* vine. Soon the huge snake was tied securely to the pole and hefted to their shoulders. As we began to move forward a spasm passed through the snake, the vines capable of tying a house together snapped as if they were string, and the burden dropped free. Again it was tied, and again the snake's involuntary twisting snapped the vines. They finally managed to get it firmly bound, climbed the hill

79

with our ungainly load, and at last emerged from the forest out into the plain.[1]

He was laid on the ground and I went for a tape measure; sixteen feet from head to tip of tail, and ten or more inches thick in the main body, except for where the antelope bulged. Out came the machetes—and at least a hundred pounds of antelope, together with his six-inch-long horns. The smell? Well, let's not talk about that.

The people were interested in the antelope, the question being, "How long has it been in there?" Local epicurean experts took into consideration how much of the hair on the skin had already peeled off, the appearance of the eyes, and other such indicators. Consensus of opinion confirmed it. The antelope had only been in the snake's stomach three days so it was still good to eat! Double blessing.

With exclamations of satisfaction, the butchering began of both snake and antelope. The people departed content with their portions. It had turned out to be a very good day indeed. Their missionary had done them a great service, bless him—though he might have had reservations on their food choice.

You might ask, "How in the world did the snake swallow an antelope with six-inch horns?" The fact of the matter is that a snake may well swallow an antelope with even longer horns which on such occasions may pierce the snake's skin. In that case we discover that the Lord invented the first self-sealing tire. The snake will simply seal the exit around the horn, finish digesting his meal, and depart in a new skin, leaving the old one lying with the horns sticking through it. And we thought the tire manufacturers were the first to come up with that idea?

I Timothy 4:4, 5 has this to say: "For every creature of God is

---

1   See the Photo Gallery on pg. 133 for a picture of the python.

80

good, and nothing to be refused, if it be received with thanksgiving: For it is sanctified by the word of God and prayer." With limited resources, our people have made the most of what's available to them.

WATCH OUT
FOR THE WILD BOAR

At our Nkole Nkema station in Congo, we had a school for the village children. Missionary schools were especially important in the jungle areas because the Belgian Colonial government did not have the resources to run schools, and so depended upon mission agencies to do the educating. In fact, in such areas if you met someone who knew how to read, they were likely taught in a parochial school. Many a teacher, preacher, mechanic, carpenter, bricklayer, cement mason, and nurse got their education through a religious organization rather than a governmental one. This was so throughout the colonial period.

And so it was that we had a number of schools scattered over the three-hundred-mile area to which we ministered. The greatest benefit and purpose was, of course, to have a literate church of folks who could read their Bibles and use song books. Otherwise they could not be truly discipled and trained to serve the God of Heaven. Taken for granted in the United States, this is an essential part of the missionary's ministry in the interior of underdeveloped nations. Our Nkole Nkema school had students from other villages which required a boarding facility as well.

Question: How do you feed a group of boys who have big appetites when there is no market or store nearby?

Answer: Buy local produce from the villagers and hunt for your own meat. The boys could go on the Saturday *djita*, the hunt with the men of our Christian village, bringing *nkosa* string nets and spears or bows and arrows.

The other way for the boys to eat meat was for me to hunt especially for them. On one occasion, Ituku and I headed out through the plain to the right of our house where it faced the road; there we might come upon an *nse* or two, swift spike-horned antelope about the size of a goat. Or maybe we would see an *nkai* (bush buck) standing waist high, beautiful in a russet coat with white stripes and spots, and crowned with eight-inch-long spiral horns. His German shepherd-like bark would announce he had spotted us and he'd wheel to run. On occasion he would stop once he was far away and bark again. Should that happen, it would take him by surprise that *Makalele Monene* could reach him with resounding effect. The people liked to say that when that gun spoke, every animal within ten kilometers ran for cover. The *nkai* would be safe today, however, because Ituku was carrying his muzzle loader so I had not brought *Makalele Monene*. I only had my Remington 550 auto-loading long rifle. I could drop an *nkai* close up with that fine gun, but we didn't often see one so close.

No matter, for today there were no *nse* in sight, nor did an *nkai* make an appearance. We entered the forest, moving with silent caution, ears alert and eyes keeping sharp watch. We heard it then— the cacophony of a group of big black *ngila*, the Calabash monkey.

"M-a-a-a-n-ko, m-a-a-a-n-ko!" they called, proud of their size and dominance. There would be *nshodjis* and perhaps *ngeis* with them; these are smaller, smarter, and more attentive monkeys who

84

make no noises that foolishly reveal where they are. They often act as sentries for the *ngilas*, whose lack of caution could cost them their lives. It was unlikely that *nkolongo* would be with them; these big red monkeys had strong, disagreeable odors that gave them away. Like the black *ngila*, they did not have much in the way of cranial "smarts" either.

Ituku and I began working our way toward the noisy *ngilas*, careful not to make a sound. Should we catch our foot in a vine, stumble over some hidden root, or move a branch or bush so that it waved, the *nshodjis* with the *ngilas* would certainly sound the alarm. We came to a stream with high banks, and it was muddy. That meant one thing only. Something big was rooting around in that stream, probably an *nshombo*, the two-hundred-pound red boar of the African jungle. Carefully, quietly, we stalked toward where the boar was feasting off succulent roots in the stream. Then we saw him, directly below us in the water.

"You can't kill him with that little gun," Ituku signed. "I'll shoot him with my muzzle loader." It was packed with black powder tamped into place and plugged with a slug of oakum. Next came the primer cap, and lastly a spear was pushed into the muzzle of the gun. Yes, I said "spear". Our hunters often took a regular-sized spear with a six- to eight-foot-long shaft and cut it to the length that would fit into their muzzle loaders. If necessary, they would shave the shaft to ensure a good fit in the barrel. They also cut the blade of the spear straight across like a chisel, sharpening that edge. This weapon, while extremely difficult to aim, would go through about anything it hit.

With that, Ituku crept up to the edge of the bank, pointed his muzzleloader at the boar, and cut loose. It was a clap of thunder in the jungle! Smoke billowed and the oakum wad flew, burning. A ferocious scream issued from the stream and an alarmed Ituku began shouting, *"Monsieur, Monsieur, beta ye, beta ye!* (Mister, Mister, shoot him, shoot him!)" Alas, Ituku had only sliced the boar's hind leg, which left him very angry. Ituku was deafened by the blast, and now a big red boar was racing past me, clashing his deadly tusks.

Now we had a scene where the missionary was racing through a tangled jungle with a .22 caliber rifle behind a wounded boar, mayhem in his eyes. Suddenly the boar realized that this white creature was chasing him, and with that he decided he was going to do the chasing. You need to understand that an African boar is one of the boldest, "baddest" animals alive. He will charge in when all others would hold back—even a leopard is much more cautious. Besides this, a boar can jump. Unless you find a good tree and get high quickly, he has been known to make a running leap and with a slash of those fearsome tusks rip a man right out of a tree.

So when he turned and charged, the chips were down. I could do nothing but stand my ground and trust God to keep that .22 from jamming. Holding it at hip level I began stitching him down the side as he came on. About six feet away the "sewing" did its job, and the big boar toppled. *Whew!*

And guess whose game it was? You're right. Ituku's, because according to their hunting rules, the man who first wounds the animal is the killer. He "generously" gave me a leg, shared it with the school boys, and we again proved that the God we serve is ever present and ever able to deliver.

"The Lord is good, a strong hold in the day of trouble; and he knoweth them that trust in him." (Nahum 1:7)

GIVING A HIPPO
A HEADACHE

Hippopotamuses are immense, attaining a weight of 2 to 4 tons and a body length of 12 to 15 feet. Their teeth are commensurate with their size. The lower canines are heavy and curved, growing up to two feet in length. The upper canines project forward and have been known to reach lengths of sixteen inches. A powerful swimmer, the hippopotamus can also walk on the bottom of a river or lake. It likes depths of ten to twelve feet for such underwater strolls; it rises to the surface for a breath every three to six minutes. Among four-footed beasts it is second in size only to the elephant. It is related to the pig and its name means "river horse".

Though usually placid, the hippo can also be extremely dangerous when in a bad mood. Louise's older brother, Bob Grings, met such a one near the village of Indolo. He needed to cross the Kasai River, and set out in a dugout canoe with the assistance of two men from Indolo. The river at that point is more than a mile wide and floods back into the jungle riverside. It was a playground for all sorts of monkeys, including a neck-less specimen with white shoulders, as well as many species of birds. Hunters shoot monkeys and birds out of the trees and paddle to where they are floating in the swamp.

Hippos like the place too, and oftentimes declare by right of force that certain areas are their domain. Canoes use these channels at their own risk. The tradeoff is obvious; the hippos love to go ashore into the manioc and banana gardens of the people, which greatly irritates the human beings and brings reprisal that often costs the hippos their lives. Besides, the meat is delicious and the hide and tusks can be sold.

The hippos sometimes pay back by attacking human beings who have the audacity to travel by canoe through what the hippos have claimed as their water and walkways. So it happened that when Bob Grings chose to pass over a "hippo highway" on his way out of the jungle into the main stream of the Kasai, Mr. Hippo was not pleased.

"Aha," he thought, "I'll teach these interlopers a lesson." Unaware of the danger awaiting them, the three men paddled the winding waterway until the canoe passed over the waiting hippo. With a lunge the monster drove his head into the bottom of the canoe, throwing the men high into the air. The hippo's great mouth gaped open, then closed on the dugout canoe, driving his tusks through the wood as if it were butter. Having impaled the canoe, his attention now turned to the men. By this time, they were scrambling up the trunks of nearby trees. Roaring, the hippo moved toward them, only to find them too high to reach. For some minutes the men stared down at the angry beast, his mouth displaying its awesome weapons and his throat speaking its displeasure. At last he submerged, a lurking submarine of potential death.

"Is he still there?" the men asked themselves. "We had better wait a while longer." Who will be first to try to reach the swamped canoe?

Brave man, the one who first entered that water. The others perspired and prayed. There—he is in the canoe, bailing. Where is that hippo? Just lurking, ready for another attack? Down from their trees and into the canoe climbed the other two men. Can you imagine the tension that twanged in the jungle air as they quietly paddled the rest of the way out of the channel and into the Kasai?

But there was a day when three hippos met more than their match. It happened when we were crossing the Kasai River by ferry at another location. Now you probably think of a ferry as a big boat with many cars and people on it, or maybe you have no mental picture at all of a ferry. This one was made up of three open metal boats pointed at both ends. The center boat contained a four-cylinder British Austin automobile engine connected to a gear box and a propeller shaft. A platform was constructed across the top of the three boats which could accommodate two trucks or four smaller vehicles. We pulled away from the landing at Brabanta and began to cross the broad Kasai. Nearing the other side we spotted three hippos directly in the path of the ferry, showing just their nostrils and eyes: Mama Hippo, Baby Hippo, and Papa Hippo. It was evident they had only one idea: *"Let's show that big boat who owns this channel."*

"Here it comes," I thought. Sure enough, as we approached the three hippos submerged. I could imagine the mother and father saying to the baby, "Now son, this is the way you do it." We passed over the spot where they had submerged. Then the metal boats of the ferry rang with two big bangs and a little one. Looking back into the wake of the ferry, we laughed as three hippos popped to the surface shaking their heads. Aspirin, anyone? And that is how you give a hippo a headache.

We can take great comfort in Isaiah 43:2. It assures us, "When thou passest through the waters, I will be with thee; and through the rivers, they shall not overflow thee."

MIDNIGHT AT MIDDAY:
EQUINOCTIAL STORMS

"Behold, I was shapen in iniquity; and
in sin did my mother conceive me."
(Psalm 51:5)

It is the changing of the seasons in tropical Africa. The four-month dry season is coming to an end, and huge, dark clouds are gathering on the eastern horizon. The air is still, as if holding its breath in fearful anticipation. Nature is quiet and waiting.

We too are on edge. Is the good lamp in a safe place? Are the hurricane lanterns ready to light? The pictures removed from the walls and stored? What is lying around that can be picked up and thrown? Where are the pots, pans, and tubs with which we catch water? Where are they? Those must be ready. Roll down the split bamboo window shutters, and make sure they are tied down with their vine strings. What is outside that needs to be brought in before the winds arrive? I hope the roof survives; the walls too, when the rain drives against their mud plaster. Have the termites weakened the structure of our house enough that it might collapse, I wonder?

The winds are beginning to blow now and the sun is buried behind a huge black blanket. The clouds are much lower and the thunder is beginning to rumble. Massive bolts of lightning are cutting jagged swaths through the tar-hued clouds. *Augh!* That bolt was right next to us. Smell the ozone! Hear that hiss. Look at the massive sheet of rain marching our way, blotting out our view of everything east of us. The first drops of rain are pelting down now, harbingers of the torrent behind them, scouts leading the way for a powerful army.

Then it is here, the first crushing blow: a wall of water driven by monstrous winds. The house is groaning; the roof is straining to loose its vine-tied moorings to the walls. A powerful gust, and then another more powerful sweeps across our little home. This storm is bent on annihilation! The thatch on the roof lifts again and again. Some layers give up the battle and roll their faces toward the sky, letting water pour through the gaps they have left. Quickly! Bring the pots and pans and tubs over here—over there. Since our house has no ceiling, every torrent pouring through the upturned thatch is launching itself upon all below.

Oh no! The window shutters have torn loose from their vine ties and are flapping wildly inside the house! Items that we left in our haste to get the most valuable things under shelter are now flying wind-driven east to west through the house. Some are bouncing off the walls; others are plastered to the walls or draped here and there over the sparse furniture. Rain blowing horizontal to the ground is flying through the windows, and everything is dripping.

C-r-a-c-k! Oh, what a searing bolt of lightning, and so near. Light the hurricane lanterns; it is dark as night inside though the clock reads noon. On the storm rages! Will it ever give up its effort to level our house? The Belgian government agent having lunch with us when the storm hit is trembling, but hanging in there as he helps where he can.

The rain begins to slacken now; the winds diminish somewhat, and the lightning is striking to the west of us. Over there the sun is beginning to peek through and the sky starts to clear. Listen; the birds and insects are chirping in chorus, joining the dripping from our roof. Distant thunder marks the retreat of an equinoctial storm—or its advance upon the next victim. At last it is quiet again; the air is filled with the freshness only a mighty storm can bring.

"I'm so glad I was here with you folks!" exclaims the Belgian, his voice filled with wonder. "I would have been terrified to death had this storm caught me in the village rest house." Newly arrived in Congo, he had never experienced the power of such a storm, and this occasion gave us an opportunity to remind him of the presence of the God of Heaven and witness to him of his need for Christ as his Savior.

Over in the native village a house lies crushed, blown to rubble by the wind and reduced to a heap of mud. It had been an old house from which the people had moved, and where they kept a hen and her chicks. In fact, the chicks had hatched just the day before and had not been outside yet. Now the mother was dead, leaving three of the chicks still alive. We took them with the idea of caring for them until they could care for themselves. In so doing we set the stage for learning a valuable spiritual lesson which became a powerful illustration of the Gospel to the people.

You see, as I said, these chicks had not yet been outside. Their mother died before having the opportunity to teach them how to scratch with their feet to turn up bugs and other food to eat. We wondered how it was going to be possible to feed chicks that did not know how to scratch. "Let's try them and see what happens," we thought. So we spread a piece of paper on the floor and scattered rice on it. Placing the three chicks on the paper in the midst of the rice, we stood back to see what would happen. Look at that! They immediately began to scratch among the grains and peck the rice with their little beaks. They already knew how to feed themselves, and did not need to be taught!

Then I thought, "What a good illustration for the people. By using something common to them we can show them that sin is inherent in our lifestyle. We can illustrate that we are born sinners. *We do not become sinners because we sin; we sin because we are sinners already in our hearts.* We already know how to scratch."

So out of a fierce storm came a helpful illustration which God used to bring conviction of sin and salvation to our jungle people.

THREATENED WITH A SPEAR

The village of Nkole Beloi was a rather unfriendly one. Not that the people were mean-spirited in general, but they were still deeply committed to the ways of the fathers and saw missionaries as intruders with a message that put the old life system at risk. Some of them in particular took strong exception to the claims of the Gospel and the transformed lives of believers in Christ. The believers had abandoned the old ways, broken the old taboos, and deserted the soothsayers, sorcerers, and medicine men. These Christians built churches in other villages and the sound of their singing, preaching, and praying reached the ears of those who would never enter a church. The missionaries would stand in the village street and preach that same message that had caused others to abandon the old life, to say nothing of the black national preachers who persistently spoke of this "new life".

Such people put the village in danger of the wrath of the spirits, which could result in sickness, death, barrenness, poor crops, lack of rain...you name it. "Leave us alone!" their thoughts shouted, and their tongues echoed the refrain. They might come to purchase soap, salt, or cloth; they might seek medical care for a wound, a terrible burn, blinding eye problems, a giant skin ulcer eating its way deep into their leg, or worm infestation. But their stay was short and their thanks brief, lest they be affected with the contagion of the white man's God. Nkole Beloi was not the only one of the thirty-six villages we reached which felt this way.

Still, we made trips as frequently as possible to Nkole Beloi and the others, sometimes by vehicle and other times by bicycle. Trips to the west through the jungle bordering the Kasai River always took us through Nkole Beloi, and we would stop to hold a Gospel service somewhere along the broad dirt street that ran through the center of the village. But few indeed responded to the offer of God's grace. Some would stop and stare for a moment, the women topless, the men clad in soiled loincloths. Others would enter their tiny huts to be out of sight.

One day I sent one of our national preachers ahead to the village of Mpombi which was well beyond Nkole Beloi on our way to Ongo and the villages farther up that road. There was school business he needed to care for there, and I would catch up to him in time to continue our journey together. Both of us were on bicycles. The road was empty. It was too late in the morning to see partridges or guinea fowl, and the antelope were bedded down somewhere in the shade of the knurled *bongondo* trees (scrub oak). The sun was beating down directly overhead, as it does only on the equator.

Glancing idly up ahead, I noticed the thin, bent figure of a man clad only in a loincloth carrying a spear. As I drew near, it became evident he was blocking the way, his spear lowered toward me. "Strange," I thought, "But perhaps he has seen game of some sort." As I came closer and finally stopped just short of his on-guard figure, I realized the game was me! With a snarl he waved the spear threateningly.

"White man," he growled, "I am going to kill you!"

Across my back was slung my .22 caliber Remington 550-A rifle, a gift from my father when he realized I needed something for small game. But what was I going to do with that to an old man waving a spear at me?

Quietly I talked to him as his eyes burned with hatred. The gall of Satan was in his heart. Lives were being changed and turning their backs upon him and his kind, who had kept them in the bondage of fear of the spirits over whom they had control. And here was one of those missionaries who was causing so many to cut the cords of the witchcraft that had bound them for so long. Here was the enemy, alone and at his mercy!

But there was one factor on which he had not counted. The missionary was not alone. It was not only the missionary here on the trail before him, but also the missionary's God. When I reminded him of that fact, he trembled and the spear lowered. His worn frame wilted, and with my Gospel challenge ringing in his ears, he turned away and I passed. After some minutes of pedaling up the road, I paused and looked back. He stood there looking at the missionary and his God—a hardened, lost old man; frail in the shimmering heat and blind in the grip of Satan.

John 3:19–20 gives God's commentary: "And this is the condemnation, that light is come into the world, and men loved darkness rather than light, because their deeds were evil. For every one that doeth evil hateth the light, neither cometh to the light, lest his deeds should be reproved."

YOU ARE NOT GOING TO DIE

Birth in Congo's jungle is an experience beyond the imagination of most folks in America. Picture, if you will, a rude one-room hut measuring 6' x 10', constructed of bark walls and a thatch roof. The floor is packed dirt, and ashes fan out from the central wood fire which is maintained at all times. The peak of the roof is a bare six feet above, and smoke rises to filter through it, leaving behind a smutty coat of carbon. Blackened tendrils of cobweb festoon here and there, and the glow of the fire is the only light available, as the hut has no windows. The single door in the side, not centered, is a small opening in the five-foot wall closed at night by a sliding shutter made of short sections of raffia palm branch stalk, tied together with vine. Be careful not to lean on anything, as you can easily become smeared with the thin layer of carbon covering everything. Over the fire in the center of the room hangs a woven reed tray about two feet square with four-inch raised sides, on which pieces of smoking monkey, antelope, or wild boar are being preserved along with fiery hot peppers called *pilipili*.

It may surprise you to learn that this dark, dirty, smoky hut is the wife's delivery room as well as her kitchen. If she dies in childbirth, the hut will be burned as cursed, and can be rebuilt at less labor and loss to the family than their larger dwelling, though made of the same materials.

When the Gospel was first preached at Nkole Nkema it created terror in the minds of the heathen leadership. Surely anyone who believed in this strange white man's god would be punished by the spirits. Certainly the spirits would zero in on the women, and any woman who became a Christian would become barren. Fear spread through the village as the terrible implications of breaking with the animism of the fathers became magnified by the cunning deception of the sorcerers, soothsayers, and witch doctors. Women under conviction of their sin and lost condition, desiring to find forgiveness, remained bound in fear by the dread of the ultimate tribal disaster: childlessness.

By God's grace, the first woman to be saved at Nkole Nkema was the mother of our pastor, Bekanga Paul. Past child-bearing age, she nevertheless was a woman and showed no evidence of being especially attacked by the evil spirits. Other women took heart and stepped across the fearsome threshold between firmly-rooted animism and faith in the Lord Jesus Christ. Out of the kingdom of darkness, into the kingdom of Light.

Then the test came. Ndongo, evangelist Njoko's wife, miscarried. A tremor of alarm felt its way through the Christian homes. Were the warnings of the heathen leadership true, or was their newfound God and Savior going to prove Himself more powerful in the end? Njoko came to let us know what had happened. Asking him what they were going to do, we expected to hear that they would resort to the old ways of going to the witch doctor and wearing fetishes tied around the wrist. Our hearts filled with praise to God as he unhesitatingly said they were through with the old ways and were committing it to the God in Whom they had put their trust.

Nketsi, evangelist Ituku's wife, was also expecting. There was no doctor to set a due date, but Nketsi had delivered two babies before becoming a Christian, and she was aware of the initial signals she was feeling. She knew it was "that time", and a knot of fear was rising within her. She was about to bring a baby into the world in opposition to generations of her people's slavery to Satan.

There was no doctor, nurse, or midwife present. According to custom, her grandmother would be in charge and other family women would help as needed. She sat on the dirt floor, her back against one of the women. It was dark, smoky, and hot in the little kitchen hut. Urgent voices were saying "*Ama, ama!* (Push, push!)", and she exerted herself, sweating and straining. Things were getting serious; something more rigorous was required.

"Bring the pepper," the grandmother said. Searing hot pepper was massaged in the birth canal. "There," she murmured, "That ought to produce the necessary action." It brought a cry of pain and lifted her up from the floor, but didn't bring the baby down.

Louise had been called, but respectful of the grandmother, had not interfered. It had been a long labor, and Nketsi was worn out. Her look of anguished pain and hopelessness was a red flag, but no one was prepared for the sudden turn when Nketsi once again groaned, "*Njo wa.* (I'm going to die.)" Often said in very difficult situations, this time was different. She had reached her limit and had indeed given up. She slumped in the arms of the woman supporting her. Her head fell backwards, and the whites of her eyes rolled up. It took a second for reality to shock Louise into action, but she jumped up from the piece of firewood on which she'd been sitting, grabbed Nketsi by her shoulders, and shook her.

Speaking sternly, she stated, "You are not going to die. Come back. You are not going to die!" A chilling silence gripped the scene; everyone was holding their breath. Life and death hung in the balance. Louise's voice penetrated the fog of exhaustion and hopelessness in Nketsi's heart and mind. An eternal moment it seemed, and then a shudder. Her head came up and her eyes rolled back as she returned from the brink. Louise held her faint gaze steady.

Desperate situations call for desperate measures. The woman supporting Nketsi clamped her hand over Nketsi's mouth and nose, robbing her of all air. In the ensuing struggle to get her breath, the baby was born. The aiding hand of the all-sufficient God reached out and instead of defeat, we were granted glorious victory. We could do nothing but thank Him and rejoice with Nketsi for her healthy boy.

"The Lord, He is God. The Lord, He is God," echoed down from Elijah's Mount Carmel that day. The curse was broken; their new-found God was more powerful than the fear of evil spirits that had ruled their people for so long. The Christian women would have babies and build Christian families. The Lord, He is God! Louise returned to our house that foggy morning knowing that she had worked shoulder to shoulder with the God of Heaven. The Lord, He is God indeed, and is "exceeding abundantly able" in every situation.

"The Lord, He is the God; the Lord, He is the God." (I Kings 18:39b)

"For in Him we live, and move, and have our being." (Acts 17:28a)

ONGO REJECTS THE GOSPEL

Located an hour's walk from the banks of the Kasai River in central Congo, Ongo is a long, narrow village with one sandy street lined with rectangular thatch-roofed huts on both sides. Beyond the far end of the village the main path forks, and the right side continues southwestward to Ntombalongo some miles further down the Kasai. The left side leads into the village, where the rest house is. The living cassava fence around the house, created by the stalks of the cassava plant, was unkempt, tall, thin, and scraggly. The gate, such as it was, slumped to one side, and the yard was filled with smelly goats, from the billy goats down to the babies. Worse— they were inside the house, and no amount of sweeping the floor and wetting it down would prevent Mark and me from having a night tormented by flea bites. The itch is most irritating, and the poison seems to take forever to leave the system. Neither was our sleep helped by the grunts and belching throughout the night by goats leaning against the bamboo slats tied with vines that masqueraded as a door.

The house was typical of the people in that particular village: slovenly, careless, lazy, and not liking whites of any description. Especially and particularly did they dislike missionaries. This was not a newly acquired attitude; Louise's family had experienced it years ago. No one in the village had ever come near to being friendly to either a missionary or his message. Vivid in my memory still is another occasion when a demon-possessed man of unspeakable filth and manner boldly entered the rest house and announced he was spending the night with me. All efforts to get him to leave were spurned, and at last he began a lewd elephant dance. Finally, I picked him up and pitched him out of the yard, over the cassava fence. Gathering himself up, he returned. "Sing," I called to Christians nearby. "Sing the songs about the blood of Jesus." Frantically he tried to chant something louder than we, but failing at that, he ran from the house, through the gate, and disappeared into the rain.

We started down the road to Ntombalongo the next day; how unspeakably sad it was to see the same demented man standing in the plain beside his house: a large termite mound dug out by a giant ant-eater. This man was living in the hollowed out stomach of the mound. No wonder his eyelids, ears, nostrils, fingers, and toes were lined with swollen pea-sized sacks created by burrowing chiggers pregnant with eggs. He was literally a living chigger factory, teeming with hundreds of them!

Again, I was back in Ongo, this time with Mark Grings. The attitude of the man responsible to see that visitors got firewood and gourds of water was typical; "long in coming and slow in doing" must have been his motto. The *kapita* (chief) was nowhere to be seen, and the *longomo* (witch doctor) sauntered around insolently. Only the children were excited by the presence of white visitors, and recognized me from previous visits. Mark and I arrived by bicycle after a twenty kilometer trip from Mpombi, where the nearest dirt road ended. Our progress had been delayed by the presence of two hippos lounging around the stick bridge that swayed its way across the swift, deep, black waters of the Diou River. We made dry season progress, crossing six smaller tributary creeks by stick bridge before the main stream. During the rainy season we would have been wading for an hour in up to waist deep water, searching for the pole bridges with our feet, by the swirl of the cross current of the creeks which flowed into the Diou.

Nor did the situation improve as the sun set and evening came on. Our attempt to hold a service was spurned by the people. No one deigned to show enough interest to come anywhere near the meeting. Many departed out of sight in evident rejection. We expected this, so continued preaching as loudly as possible, calling upon those out there behind the houses to listen to the message of the Lord Jesus Christ.

We left the next morning after securing porters to carry our box to the next village, down the road to the southwest. Ntombalongo was at the end of the road, and we were welcomed by villagers open to the Gospel and a group of Christians in the early stages of forming a church. Their enthusiasm for the things of God was a blessing, as was the delicious meal made for us by the wife of one of the Christians. We had killed a couple guinea fowl on the way, plump birds about the size of a nice chicken, decked in blue feathers with white spots. She prepared a *botumu*[1], which being interpreted is a pressure cooked jungle meal. After cutting the bird into portions, she placed them in the center of a special kind of large leaf. After adding salt, a couple of hot peppers, some sweet yellow palm oil, and a little water, she folded the leaves up around the meat and tied them together at the top with a small vine. She now had an airtight bundle which she hung over a low fire all night long. It was indeed a jungle pressure cooker! Oh, the

---

1   Pronounced *bot-oo-moo*

aroma when we opened it to eat with boiled cassava. She had made her family one as well with the bird we'd given her, so everyone was well satisfied.

A less pleasant aspect of Ntombalongo was the presence of myriads of mosquitoes. Built on the banks of the Kasai River, the village was a breeding place for these small pesky predators. "Early to bed" was the rule, for at sundown clouds of them appeared looking for dinner, and unless we were on our cots under our mosquito nets by that time, *we* were sure to be *their* feast.

Ministry completed, we returned to Ongo for another night on our way back to our station at Nkole Nkema. The men we secured at Ongo to carry our equipment to Mpombi had different ideas about their responsibility. We discovered what they had in mind halfway along the trail, for there we found our stuff sitting beside the path. A certain problem now presented itself. How were we going to manage two bicycles, the .22 rifles slung across our backs, *and* a metal foot-locker box with camp cots tied on top? It appeared Ongo thought this might indicate that we should decide this visit to them was our last. But such was not the case, as you will read in the next story. Galatians 6:9 admonishes, "Let us not be weary in well doing: for in due season we shall reap, if we faint not." And God did indeed have a reaping time for us.

A MIRACLE AT ONGO

We were blessed to have three national traveling evangelists working with us to reach our region of thirty-six villages with the Gospel. One of these, Yakobo, mainly traveled into the west and southwest areas. On many occasions he had crossed the Kasai River to the south side and returned to report villages that had never heard the Gospel.

Of necessity, Yakobo frequently passed through the village of Ongo. Always the result was the same: utter rejection. Sometimes he would go from there directly across the Kasai, which entailed a thirty minute walk to the bank of the river and another thirty minutes being paddled in a dugout canoe through the maze of trees that stood in the waters of a swamp. The area was alive with water-loving monkeys, crocodiles, and hippos.

One day, when Yakobo had been away for several weeks, we saw him turning his bicycle into our U-shaped dirt driveway. He seemed to be in a hurry and especially energized, and we wondered what had him excited.

"*Monsieur, monsieur okondima yango te, okondima yango te* (Sir, sir, you will not believe it)!"

107

"*Kondima nini te* (Not believe what)?" was my rejoinder. Then the almost unbelievable news reached my ears.

"Twelve people confessed the Lord Jesus as their Savior last night at Ongo!"

Incredible!

"Get ready to return with me, Yakobo. We're going back."

And go back we did, on that long familiar trail over which we had returned again and again sick at heart over the utter lostness and blindness of Ongo. At that time, the Mpombi section of the road was impassable to our Chevrolet Carryall, so extra miles were added to our journey. As a result it was after dark when we dragged ourselves, exhausted, into the village. Finding just an empty hut to stay in, I set up my camp cot and hung the mosquito net. By the light of my little kerosene hurricane lantern I mixed an instant pudding with canteen water for my supper, too tired for any other effort. It had been much too late to attempt holding a service, so I prepared to go to sleep. Crawling under my mosquito net, I opened my Bible to read. Was that a cough at the low doorway of the hut? Indeed, it was.

"Who?" I called.

"It's me," came the answer.

"And who is me?" I asked.

"I have come to receive Christ as my Savior," the person responded. With that I came out of my mosquito net and invited the seeking one inside.

No sooner had that newly-born again child of God left the hut that another came. And another, and another...until by 2 a.m., when the last one left rejoicing, thirty-two newborn babes in Christ had been added to the family of God in Ongo. What a night of rejoicing! God had at last moved in power in the village of Ongo. We spent the next day studying the Word of God together, building the foundation in each life for the glory of God.

From that glorious beginning, the church at Ongo grew rapidly under the leadership of Pastor Ilonga, one of our trained preachers from Nkole Nkema. On my next visit to Ongo, I found a church building standing in a new, all-Christian village. To my amazement the Christians were holding daily morning devotions in the church at sunup, in addition to the Wednesday evening prayer meeting and two Sunday services. What a sight to see them running to church at 6 a.m. at the sound of the drummer calling "Yaka na losambo" and "Teitu londo" ("Come to church," in Lingala and Lonkutu). They were running at 6 a.m. to make sure they were not late! Incredible! It was at that time they requested for my whole family to come.

We planned the family visit carefully. David and Jonathan could ride on the crossbar of a couple of men's bicycles, and Deborah would be carried in a "papoose sling" over one of our shoulders while we rode our bikes on the trail. Word was sent to the Ongo Christians that we were coming on a certain day.

We headed for Mpombi as appointed; the road was now cleared of fallen trees and the washed-out places were repaired. Twenty kilometers later after a picturesque jungle drive, we pulled into Mpombi and were greeted by the folks involved in the Christian school and church there.

Then a very strange thing happened. As we were preparing to mount our bicycles to begin the next part of the journey, we heard chanting—the rhythmic chanting that characterizes men carrying a burden together. Down where the trail to Ongo exited the village, we saw a group of men appear carrying a *kipoi* (a stick seat tied to two long poles). This was the normal manner in which they carried government officials. Chanting they came, until stopping in front of us, they lowered the *kipoi* to the ground.

"Where are you headed?" I asked.

"We came to carry your wife and daughter to Ongo," was their reply.

"Oh, no, that can't be." I responded, "We wouldn't expect you to do that."

"But that is why we came," they stated. "We wish to do it." They had told us previously they wanted to do so, but to us it had seemed unthinkable.

So Louise sat in the *kipoi*, cradling little Deborah, and was carried much of the way to Ongo. When we arrived, they lowered her with a flourish in front of a hut specially prepared for us. Bananas, plantains, papayas, cassava, and other food items were lined across the front. We were speechless.

Gaining my voice at last, I asked, "What can we pay you?"

"Nothing," they responded. "You see, you have already paid us. When we spurned you, treated you like dogs, cursed you, walked away from the preaching of the Gospel, and in spite of everything we did you kept coming back, you kept taking it...

"When you kept on preaching the message of salvation to us until, at last, we began to listen and God turned us from our sin to Himself...

"Missionary, you have already paid us!"

And so took place the miracle of Ongo, another demonstration of the love and power of the great God whom we serve. Romans 1:16, fulfilled in the 19th century:

"The Gospel of Christ...the power of God unto salvation to everyone that believeth."

HER REASONABLE SERVICE

Editor's note: The previous story covers a lengthy timeline which began with the salvation of many Ongo villagers and continued to the point at which the Christians had become so numerous that the opposition and persecution they experienced as a result forced them to build a separate Christian village. This story falls in the middle of this timeline: after that first group of villagers had come to Christ, but before the Christian village had been built.

The village of Ongo held a long standing hatred and fear of the Gospel of the Lord Jesus Christ, which was not eliminated by the glorious salvation of more than forty of its villagers. On the contrary, it was intensified as the village leadership sought to nullify the effects of the Christians' new lives. Because of the witch doctor's control over the village hunting—he would seek the direction of the evil spirits as to where the hunts ought to take place—it was immediately recognized that Christian men should not go on those hunts.

Under the leadership of Evangelist Ituku and his wife Nketsi, the singing, preaching, and praying of the Christians were a constant irritation to the unsaved. The old ways of evil spirit worship, communication with the dead, rampant sexual promiscuity, and the involvement of witchcraft in every facet of life could in no way be made compatible with the new life in Christ being experienced by the Christians. Pressure from the heathen leadership, attempts to bring the Christians back under the rule of Satan, and the believers' growing understanding of their new life soon led to an inevitable conclusion. The Christians must build their own Christian village.

As these pressures were building, what proved to be a dark cloud appeared on the horizon of Ituku and Nketsi's life. Nketsi was once again expecting a baby. You will remember Ongo was not their home village. They were from our station at Nkole Nkema and it was there that Nketsi had been God's means of breaking the back of the insidious Satanic campaign to convince women not to become Christians because they would then be barren due to their failure to follow the old ways of animism. Our story "You Are Not Going to Die"[1] tells of the dramatic intervention of God in Nketsi's near death experience with her previous baby. But now they were living miles from home in the village of Ongo and far from Louise's help which had been used of God for Nketsi's deliverance.

We advised Ituku and Nketsi to take a short furlough from their work at Ongo and have the baby at our Nkole Nkema station and Christian village, but dedication to their people at Ongo kept them from taking that step. The day came and labor ensued. It was difficult—too difficult. Ituku and Nketsi prayed. The Ongo Christians prayed fervently, and God heard. But the Lord had other plans for Nketsi; she, Ituku, and all the village Christians were going to learn that our God is indeed omnipotent and loving, but He is also sovereign and has thoughts different than our thoughts. God speaks in

---

1 Pg. 99

Isaiah 55:8–9, "For my thoughts are not your thoughts, neither are your ways my ways, saith the Lord. For as the heavens are higher than the earth, so are my ways higher than your ways, and my thoughts than your thoughts."

So it was on that day the Sovereign God of the universe called one of His dear children home to glory, and left a grieving husband and a group of young believers better able to understand that this God, the Creator God of the universe, has nothing in common with fetishes, amulets, charms, and idols. This is the God in whose hands His people's lives rest, to be either lived or taken for His glory as their "reasonable service." (Romans 12:1)

On the human level we wondered, "Would it have been different at Nkole Nkema?" No, for she had lived at Nkole Nkema for the glory of God to teach both heathens and believers alike that the Lord, He is God, and that their charms and incantations could not seal up the womb of the women believers. She had given her earthly life at Ongo to honor Him in another way, as a willing sacrifice to His purpose and His cause. In both places God was honored and glorified, God's people were edified, and His servant Nketsi served Him, even to the giving of her life.

Her grave at Ongo, also containing the unborn baby, stood as a monument to the courage and sacrifice of a servant of the Most High God. A common woman from a backward people had joined the ranks of God's special folk.

Ilonga and his wife Mpembe replaced Ituku[2] at Ongo and it was under their leadership that the new Christian village was built. Poles, vines, and palm branch thatch were cut in the forest, plots were

---

2   Ituku returned to Nkole Nkema and later remarried. Twenty-five years later when the Champlins returned to Congo for a visit, he was still faithfully living for the Lord.

cleared in the grassy plain, and soon houses stood on either side of the wide dirt street. A church went up. Five days a week, at 6a.m. and again in the evening, the people gathered to worship the glorious Sovereign God of the universe. Saturdays the men went to the forest for their own weekly hunt. Sunday they again packed the church to capacity. The miracle of Ongo glowed ever brighter, the Shekinah of God shining upon a jungle people, and it was marvelous in our eyes.

"I beseech you therefore, brethren, by the mercies of God, that ye present your bodies a living sacrifice, holy, acceptable unto God, which is your reasonable service." (Romans 12:1)

A LESSON IN ANIMISM

"For the invisible things of him from the
creation of the world are clearly seen,
being understood by the things that are
made, even his eternal power and Godhead;
so that they are without excuse..."
(Romans 1:20)

Picture a man who had been lovingly nursed back to health by missionaries after being severely injured. Can you imagine that, after returning to his village a mile away, he refused to ever speak to them again? It would likely be difficult for you to accept that, but this might indicate you need to understand animism and the history and culture of Africa.

"Animism? What is animism?" You ask. Well, let us begin with a little background, for you cannot understand it unless you are familiar with some African history.[1]

First, remove writing from the picture. No black African people ever developed and put into use a written language.

Second, remove accurate history from the scope of your thinking, for all African records are oral and largely mythical. To the African,

---

1   Much of the content here is gleaned from a combination of John S. Mbiti's book *African Religions & Philosophy* and my personal missionary experience.

the essential question about history is not "Is it accurate?" but, "Does it explain what we are and why we are what we are?"

Third, remove any great African prophet from the landscape. Africa produced no prophets because Africans had no word for "everlasting" or "eternal" in any of their three thousand languages before missionaries brought the concept to them. With no eternity to look forward to, a great golden future such as a prophet would present never "evolved" over the centuries from the thoughts and experiences of the African people. Their religions exist as a combination of oral traditions, myths, legends, and practices.

Africans recognize that there is a great Creator God who might be described in eleven words: good, merciful, holy, omnipotent, omniscient, omnipresent, limitless, self-existent, spirit, unchangeable, and unknowable. This God is indeed great, but not *immanent*. That is to say, He is not present or accessible. Because the great God is inaccessible, they have added to Him innumerable other spirit-beings. And it is these beings with whom they communicate through prayers, sacrifices, offerings, singing, dancing, fetishes, and ceremonies.

To many Africans, the sun, moon, stars, rain, storms, wind, thunder, lightning, and rainbows are deities. Also there are the nature spirits: the earth, hills, mountains, rocks and boulders, trees and forests, metals, lakes, ponds, rivers, waterfalls, rapids, lagoons, and river banks. Some diseases and even death itself are considered to be nature spirits which have human-like characteristics. Animism is basically the practice of attributing spiritual presences to both animate and inanimate objects, and then worshipping and giving obeisance and service to those objects and the spirits they believe reside in them.

Disembodied human spirits are also heavily involved in the daily life of the African. Spirits of the recent dead are contacted on a regular basis at altars where an offering of food or drink is laid and the spirits are spoken to by name. These are called the "living dead", for they are immortal so long as they are remembered by someone calling them by name and visiting them at an altar. For spirits fortunate enough to have had a large extended family through grandfathers, grand-mothers, uncles, aunts, wives, and children, this could go on for five generations. The living remember and communicate with the dead in four different ways:

1) Offering food and drink at shrines

2) Consulting medicine men, mediums, and diviners

3) Praying through them as intermediaries to God

4) Naming children after the dead

Spirits of the long-since dead who make contact with the living are called ghosts and are regarded with great fear as ill omens. These ghosts are no longer voluntarily contacted by living people who know their names, or brought offerings at an altar where the living can talk with them.

Death has four reasons:

1) Sorcery, witchcraft, and evil magic

2) Offended spirits

3) Curses and broken taboos

4) Natural causes such as accident or sickness; however, death is *rarely* attributed to such causes. An evil spirit is surely behind the incident.

Mothers hope the births of their babies will go well because of their observance of dietary and other taboos, the performance of rituals, the making of offerings, the wearing of charms and amulets, and the consultations with medicine men and diviners concerning any problems. Protection is sought from magic, sorcery, witchcraft, evil eye, disease, and evil spirits. Amulets are prepared for the mother and baby by medicine men and diviners. An amulet is a bundle of spiritually powerful substances tied to the mother and her child. Sometimes mothers give their children animal names in hopes of deceiving the spirits who might otherwise attack the baby.

Medicine men, either male or female, may spend many years learning the names and natures of herbs, trees, roots, seeds, bones, bird and animal droppings, and other natural substances. They treat physical diseases with such herbal medicines, some of which are of real value. They also treat psychological problems with sorcery, witchcraft, magic, evil spirits, curses, and other types of incantations. Most illnesses and troubles are ascribed to magic, sorcery, witchcraft, broken taboos, or the work of the spirits.

Diviners also work as medicine men. They deal with the question of finding out "why" something has gone wrong. Bones, hair, and other body parts may be used as tools in this divination. Germs may exist for the modern thinker, but someone or something puts the germs on the one who becomes ill.

Mediums are people who are believed to possess the ability of getting in touch with the spirit world at will.

Seers work with psychic powers; they have a great potential for communication with demonic spirits, whom they most often think to be spirits of departed human beings.

Ritual elders take charge of the performance of rituals in their communities.

Rainmakers are trained in weather observation, movements in the sky, habits of insects, birds, and certain animals, as well as plants and trees. They practice rain-making rituals and are extremely important individuals in the agricultural societies of Africa.

Only natural disasters are beyond the scope of African medicine. These are thought to be acts of God, who can do as He pleases, and for such matters they pray to Him. Everything else is within the ken of their animistic African religion.

Key to African thought is that all sickness and calamity, outside of major natural disasters, are *put on them by someone or something*. That something or someone must be discovered and warded off with the amulets, medicines, or fetishes supplied by the medicine men with the assistance of the seer, the diviner, the medium, the ritual elder...

With this background in mind, let us continue to the story of Bakula.

MAULED BY A LEOPARD

Bakula was muscular and about five feet seven in height; he was just an average hunter in an average *djita*. But what was lurking in the jungle was anything but average, and Bakula's protective amulet was about to be tested to the limit and found wanting. As was customary, Bakula's hunt began with consulting the local witch doctor, whose duty it was to communicate with the spirits to find out from them at what location in the jungle the village men will have the best success in hunting. The witch doctor's reward is the best cut of the booty.

What a motley crew emerged from the village! Around their loins they wore *mpekwa*, cloth woven from raffia palm tree fibers. When it was new, the cloth had been cream in color, but smoke and sweat had darkened it and the red *ngola* wood powder used for body painting had added ocher to the mix along with plenty of dirt. The smell of wood smoke followed the men, wafting naturally from their hair and bodies because of the little fires kept burning ceaselessly in the tiny mud and stick dwellings where they had spent the night. Had it been a man or a pair of men out hunting elephant with spears, their bodies would have been smeared with elephant droppings. But these men

121

were after other game and so were *au naturel*. Somewhere on their bodies, perhaps their necks, wrists, or ankles, were the most important part of their garb and equipment: their amulets. These bundles of magical substances and resident spirit power were their protection from the myriad dangers, both physical and spiritual, which lurked in the forest. Such dangers could take the form of deadly snakes, brutally powerful wild boars which could leap high and tear fleeing men out of the trees, or the fearsome leopard—just to name a few.

About half of the hunters had jungle fiber nets slung over their shoulders, anchored at either end by five-foot-long hardwood stakes with sharpened ends. Stretched, the nets would contribute about fifty feet per man to the total net being used in the hunt. They also carried bows and arrows or spears; the other half of the men were equipped with weapons as well but carried no nets.

Into the jungle they marched, the expert trackers and guides at the forefront. On occasion the hunt could entail an entire day's march, depending on its intended purpose. Were it near the end of the year and the village needed to sell meat in order to pay their annual "head tax" to the colonial government, the hunt might last for a week or more. In such cases, they would penetrate deep into the jungle. In Bakula's case, however, a short march sufficed. Through the tangled jungle and across a stream and swampy area they hacked their way until the leader signaled, "This is the place"—the place where the spirits, through the witch doctor, had said the hunt would be good.

One after another the net men drove their stakes into the ground, end to end with the net of the man just ahead. In the gloom of the jungle the woven fibers blended into the background and become just a part of the scenery. As the trap was being set, the other men circled out to form a pie shape of drivers whose purpose it was to frighten the animals between them and the nets; the animals would flee into the nets where they would await death.

I experienced such a *djita* with the men from our Christian village (no communication with spirits, of course) and was armed with my double recurve bow. I remember the thrill of excitement when I heard the thundering hooves of a big black *mbende* antelope heading toward me. Hiding behind a big tree, I drew my bow to the limit and held it. Loosing the arrow just as the tip of the large antelope's nose appeared, I was rewarded with a perfect strike and a prize which dropped within a few yards. But that is another story.

The stage was now set. The nets were in place and the drivers began their push through the jungle. Shouting, stomping, and clanging their file-sharpened machetes against the trees, the men set up a clamorous din that echoed through the jungle. Hornbills squawked and lifted off the treetops in alarm. Monkeys chattered to one another as they hastened from the racket. Antelope pricked up their ears, raised their tails, and dashed headlong from the noise. The thud of their hooves was music to the ears of the men waiting at the net. The big red wild boar grunted his aggravation and clacked his tusks, a note of anger mixed with his apprehension. Alerted to the need for escape, his troop followed him toward the unseen nets, where their arrival would cause a few anxious moments to the men hiding there.

Gliding in haste but not in panic, a leopard also moved toward the nets. His muscles rippled under his smooth fawn coat, dappled with black spots. He weighed more than two hundred pounds and measured perhaps thirty inches tall at the shoulder and eight feet long including his tail, which was now twitching with annoyance. Fetid breath sifted through his teeth as the distinctively sweet smell of humans reached his nostrils. Eyes bright, their light-gathering faculties at high alert, the leopard eased to a stop. The humans were just ahead, located by his nose as well as if they stood in plain view rather than crouched behind the trees. His keen vision picked out the nets, standing in bold relief against the jungle backdrop.

"I'll go back toward the noise," he decided—and pity any human beings he meets on his way. Every sense on alert, his determination for escape lending added power to his movements, the leopard turned toward the oncoming men. Flitting noiselessly from sun to shade to shadow, his coloring rendering him virtually invisible, the fearsome figure glided through the forest.

Bakula was there, continuing his racket-making and shouting now and then, "There goes an *mbende* (or *nkulupa* or *mengia*) toward the nets!" He and others of the beaters yelled out these warnings for the net minders to signal the approach of various jungle antelope. Here and there one of the men caught a little terrier-sized *mboloko* antelope (dik-dik) as it ran helter-skelter in confusion. This little fellow would be eaten in totem, even the contents of its stomach and intestines, which made a complete meal of meat and vegetables.

Ahead of the beaters the first antelope had plunged into the nets, tangling its hooves and horns in a desperate attempt to escape before dying under the spears of the men who rushed from their places of hiding. Then the pack of wild boars appeared, charging wildly in a scattered group but somehow always sensing the leader's location. With a shrieking squeal he led them into the center of the net, his head swinging and his great tusks shredding the net. Brave men entered the melee as the boars streamed through the hole, and several fell to their spears. Here and there a man would launch an *njika*, a barbed arrow constructed out of two pieces with a strong cord attached to the head. The cord, stretched between the arrow head and shaft, would soon hook onto a small tree, vine, or jungle plant. The boar would struggle to pull loose, only to find the hunter had followed his impeded progress and arrived in time to finish the kill with his spear.

Continuing to glide away from the nets toward the drivers, the special smell of an approaching human filled the leopard's nostrils. He paused, his glowing yellow eyes wide as Bakula filled the field of his vision. The enemy was approaching, oblivious to the leopard's presence.

Suddenly the leopard hurtled in Bakula's direction, his roar of rage ringing in the man's ears. Like a missile launched, the leopard's leap carried it directly toward Bakula, his first bound covering half of the distance. For another hunter who was quicker of reflex and braver of heart, there might have been time to lower his spear and meet the leopard's charge. But for Bakula, his faith in the protective amulet forgotten and his legs turned to water by a cascade of fear screaming *"Run!"* it was already too late. He wheeled around in desperate flight, but the leopard's second leap brought him down upon Bakula's back.

The claws of his right paw encircled Bakula's head. One sharp curve entered the corner of his left eye. Another passed through his nose and a third pierced the roof of his mouth. Two others buried themselves deep in his scalp. His garbled screams, mixed with the leopard's roar, alerted Bakula's fellow hunters to his plight and they rushed toward him through the tangled jungle. The leopard had Bakula by the arm now, his teeth holding him helpless and his claws deep into the flesh. His back legs and their fearsome power were just coming into play. Cries of anger and fear filled the air as the men arrived. Releasing his victim, the leopard turned to face his assailants and found them too many to defeat; a hail of spears soon dispatched him.

The jungle grew quiet again except for the sounds of the hunters gathering the spoils of their hunt, rolling up their nets, and beginning the trek back toward their village. The animals which had escaped stood trembling, birds roosted once again in the tree tops, monkeys returned to their food gathering, and prowlers began once again their ceaseless hunt for food as the sounds of the invading humans receded into the distance.

Back at Nkole Nkema the villagers were first alerted to Bakula's plight by the chanting of the hunters returning. Bakula appeared, torn and bloody but walking. Especially brave and skilled he was not, but he was certainly tough. Like other badly wounded men, he had followed the custom of coming in on his own two feet. So it was that he appeared at our mission station that evening, accompanied by men who told his tale. What a sight!

Antiseptic poured into the bite wound on his left arm ran through and out the other side. Carefully we cleaned the many claw wounds, including those through his nose, mouth, and the corner of his eye. God had been merciful to him, for those claws a little to one side or the other could have cost him his sight. He remained stoic, saying little. We repeated the dressings until his wounds healed.

Strange—he never uttered a word of thanks. No conversation. No response to our speaking of the grace, love, and mercy of God that had been extended to him, not just in this instance but also—especially—upon the cross of Calvary. Then he came no more.

We looked for him in the village on our frequent visits for Gospel services and other business with the people. Now and then we would see him, but always he would move away when we turned toward him. At last it dawned on us that he was ashamed. Ashamed of the failure of his amulets to protect him. Ashamed of his lack of courage. Above all, ashamed of having been obligated by the circumstances to seek the white man's help when his ancestors' gods and resources had failed him.

Once again the powerful hold of animism and the deception of Satan reminded us of the truth of Romans 1:19–21.

"Because that which may be known of God is manifest in them; for God hath shewed it unto them. For the invisible things of him from the creation of the world are clearly seen, being understood by the things that are made, even his eternal power and Godhead; so that they are without excuse: Because that, when they knew God, they glorified him not as God, neither were thankful; but became vain in their imaginations, and their foolish heart was darkened."

Praise God that power was broken by the grace of God in many, many other individuals as is illustrated in these stories time and again!

BECOMING A MAN

The pale golden glow of the rising sun on the jungle horizon reveals an unearthly sight. What are those young men doing wrapped in vines, arms and legs around tree trunks, clinging as if their life depended on it? Why have they spent hours on those tree trunks desperately afraid of dropping off from exhaustion while being whipped by older men and verbally abused with insults to their strength and courage? Why?

"They are candidates for initiation into the exclusive Nkanga Society," a village authority would answer. The test was designed to prove the qualities of nerve and physical strength expected in a real man, not just a male of the species. Now they are going to be chased with whips back into the village for another, more painful step toward that prized membership in the Nkanga Society. Here they come, running wildly through the brush, the whip men hard on their heels. Panting, they stream into the village.

A great crowd is gathered in Nkole Nkema's wide dirt street that separates the two long rows of bark and stick houses comprising the village. The excitement is electric. The young men work to screw up their courage, hearts beating fast and strong. Mothers steel themselves for what is coming. Their fathers stand stoic and apprehensive. *The* day has arrived. A day looked forward to with both hope and fear. Will these teenage boys prove themselves to be men or reveal their boyish weakness? Can they take it, or will they struggle to be free? Will their mothers survive either the terror of seeing their sons so severely tested or the shame of having them relegated to "less-than-a-man" status?

Moving with the crowd to the scene upon which every thought of the village focuses, we see loincloth-clad men preparing the test. Red hot *pilipili* (peppers), about the size of the tip of your little finger, have been dried in the sun and are now being pounded into a fine powder mixed with rock salt in a small wooden mortar. They mix the concoction with water. Another man molds pliable leaves into small funnels.

The would-be men arrive, bodies glistening with the sweat of their race and dread of severe pain. Already their mothers have begun a low warbling moan, vicariously sharing in the coming pain.

"Lie down here," a voice commands.

Dutifully the young men lie down bare-backed on the sandy dirt. The mothers' wails rise as the leaf funnels are inserted into the young men's nostrils. The pitch goes up a notch again as the men in charge of the ceremony approach with the mixture of powdered pepper and salt.

The leaf funnels fill and empty and fill and empty again as the fiery mixture pours into the nostrils and sinuses of the teenage boys.

Tears flood from their closed eyes. Abdominal muscles spring rigid; toes curl on convulsed legs. Fingers dig deep into the soil. Hearts pound in time with the screaming pain. Courage rises as every thought is locked on the goal...no struggle, no sound, *be a man, a man, a man.*

Mothers now are rolling on the ground crying and screaming for them. Fathers stand, muscles tensed, remembering the pain, the pressure to pass the test—remembering when they became a man. Others watch and remember when they failed the test and were excluded, as they are now, from the society and privileges of manhood.

Nostrils and sinuses are swollen, but the pain is contained now as the caustic effect of the pepper and salt begins to wane. "I'm a man"— the thrill of it races through the victors. "He's a man," shout the hearts of their mothers, and the fathers nod; "He's a man." Another generation of men has entered the life stream of the village. Watch as those who passed the test rise in the glow of victory. Notice others who failed slink off in their shame.

But we who have higher goals remember Paul's words to the Corinthians in his first epistle, "They do it to obtain a corruptible crown; but we an incorruptible." (I Corinthians 9:25)

Bravely they passed the earthly test. Ours is far more challenging. We will stand before the Judge of the whole earth to determine if we've run our race with certainty and may obtain the plaudit of the One for Whom we've kept our body "under."

PHOTO

GALLERY

Above: Church's farewell to Champlins in Los Angeles, 1954
Upper right: Little David, during the Champlins' trek across the States
prior to leaving for Congo in 1954
Lower right: Family at Nkole Nkema

Upper left: Carrying an elephant skull

Lower left: The boys with an *mbende* antelope

Right: Darrell with the elephant he shot (Rogue Elephant)

Below: Darrell, David, and Jonathan with the python
Darrell shot

Upper right: The Champlin family, Christmas of 1959

Lower right: A large fruit bat

Left: Hunters carrying a leopard

Right: A witchdoctor

Left: Darrell at Nkole
Nkema

Right: Darrell with his
Cape buffalo

Top left: Darrell on the path to Ongo.

Bottom left: The village of Ongo.

Top right: The church family at Ongo; Ilonga Petelo on the far right.

PrePare immediately To evacuate. Situation grim, Helicopter coming. Don'T delay. Don'T question! Kandala burned. Missionaries in danger. Helicopter will Return. Roads dangerous. GeT ouT by helicopter. Everyone must geT ouT. Mim also.
Irene is dead. STay on sTaTion. waiT FoR helicopter. Love, DARRell

A replica of the bandage message dropped (Terror in Congo, pg. 258). The piece of torn sheet was about two yards long and four inches wide with an 18-inch tear at the end.

WHITE MAN, DO YOU EAT SNAKE?

One of the great hurdles for our Congo Christians to surmount has always been the "*makambo na Bankoko*", the things of the fathers, such as *ndoki* (witchcraft) and *bikila* (taboos). The *ndoki* is not extremely difficult because it is plain to them as Christians that witchcraft is of Satan, a very evident evil. The problem when dealing with witchcraft is not recognizing it as evil, but rather the price one pays in the animosity and the sometimes violent reactions of those who practice it.

But taboos, being so thoroughly interwoven with their personal life style and psyche, are another matter. If you had been taught from childhood, for instance, that anyone in your family who eats any chicken product will certainly fall ill, you might have difficulty eating chicken or eggs. These are not matters of taste. It is not that they don't like this or that, such as might be the case with Americans who are picky about food. For instance, I love okra and eggplant any way they are fixed, but our children would rather not see them on their plates at any time. Taste buds determine likes and dislikes, but that is not what we are talking about when we discuss African taboos.

Taboos go back for generations in families and clans. No one in a family will eat a particular fish, bird, or whatever, once an oath or curse is pronounced involving the item. Women in the Bankutu tribe were taught from childhood that something terrible would happen to them if they ate anything containing chicken, the big black *mbende* antelope of the jungle, or the brainless black *ngila* monkey. They had never questioned the taboo, so when I joked with them that the men were deceiving the women because those were the most easily procured meats and the men wanted them all to themselves, they were taken aback.

Sometimes a society will have a special taboo. To the Nkanga, it was a little fish of the same name found in jungle streams. When joining the society they pronounced an oath, swearing that eating the *bokanga* fish would result in certain death. It was not an easy society to enter[1]. Suffice it here to say that in such a society, taboos become almost part of their genes, pervading their thoughts and lifestyle.

Then came Christ and the Bible. II Corinthians 5:17 says, "If any man be in Christ, he is a new creature: old things are passed away; behold, all things are become new," and this took on a very definite cultural meaning. So integral is obedience to the Bible in this area, so meaningful to Christians in their own understanding of the clarity of their faith, that it became part of the proof of their salvation. In effect, they concluded that if they did not have faith to believe that God would protect them from the consequences of breaking their taboos, then they had not truly put their trust in Christ. Rather, it was still placed in some lesser god who was not superior to those they had bowed to in their heathenism. Baptismal candidates were (are) required to eat their taboo as proof of their faith in Christ, evidence of truly being a new creation in Christ and old things having passed

1   "Becoming a Man", pg. 129

away. To them it was obvious that someone not truly saved would never dare break their taboos in order to be baptized.

This test of faith began early in the history of our people's Christianity. In fact, our great pastor, Bekanga Paul, may well have driven the thought home to them when he boldly broke the taboos of the Nkanga society. He, Ituku, Ndjoku, and Iyende were progressing as leadership in the church at Nkole Nkema. When it became clear to Bekanga that it was a shame upon the name of Christ to keep this taboo because of fear of the reprisal brought by the oath or the demon spirits before whom the oath had been taken, he determined to take action. Calling the other men, he presented each of them with one of the little *bokanga* fish. In front of them he swallowed his whole, in the name of the Lord Jesus Christ. His Lord would protect him! The other men followed, but with some trepidation.

He laughed as he told me of Ituku coming to his house in the middle of the night, calling, "Bekanga, Bekanga, my stomach hurts!"

Bekanga's response was, "Go back to sleep, Ituku. Trust your Lord." When they awoke hale and hearty the next morning, they knew that God was indeed God.

With that, the dam broke. Edibles formerly shunned became a part of the Christians' diet, to the disbelief and disgust of the unsaved. The Christians really rubbed the fur the wrong way when they began killing and eating the civet cat (*ebonde*). These cats, about sixteen inches tall at the shoulder, were fat from stealing chickens from home roosts (chicken pens or houses were not built), catching ground nesting birds and rodents, and munching on the delicious pineapples behind people's houses. These nocturnal cats were not the smartest little animals and could be killed easily on moonlit nights simply by meeting them on a path and standing stock still in the shade of a *bongondo* tree until the *ebonde* came close enough to club. In fact, Nsimba Mputu told me of an occasion when he was out on such a night and saw one of them coming. It swung from one side of the path to the other, sniffing for a rodent or bird. Standing shaded but having nothing with which to club it, he was going to have some fun with it. The cat actually came up to his feet and began sniffing.

"*Boo!*" he shouted. The cat rolled onto its back growling, its feet fanning in the air until at last it flipped over and dashed into the grass.

Not only were these civet cats easy to kill, but they were good to eat. On the other hand, this activity did not meet with the approval of the unsaved villagers, and in particular the *longomo* (witch doctor). There would be reprisal against someone killing and bringing a civet cat into the village, and sometimes the Christians carried them through the heathen village on their way home. That had to stop.

So it came about when I was in the village one day, I was approached by a *longomo*. The conversation went something like this.

"Missionary, I want you to forbid your believers to carry civet cats through this village. They are polluting the village with this taboo animal and will bring sickness and death upon us."

"Ah," I said, "You won't die if you eat that animal. Our people have found it's not only easy to kill but good to eat."

"White man," he asked, "Do you eat snake?"

"Well, no," I answered.

"You see," he replied, "You white people have taboos just like us blacks."

Now the fat was in the fire. "Do you mean that you as a black man would eat civet cat if I as a white man would eat snake?"

"Yes, that is what I mean," stated the *longomo*.

"It's a deal, sir," I responded, and walked away wondering how I was going to meet his challenge.

A day or two later Bekanga Paul went hunting. Passing in front of our house, he continued on the trail back through the plains and into the jungle. Hours later he returned, his bow and arrows in one hand and a machete in the other. On his back, strapped in place with lengths of pliant bark, was his *botete*, a flat half-basket made from a frame of woven palm branches. Something was packed into the *botete*.

"What do you have there, Bekanga?" I called.

"An *mboma*," he responded. A python! It was exactly what I needed.

"How did you get it?" I inquired.

"Didn't see anything to shoot," he replied, "But I stopped on the way back to cut some *mbongo* leaves (they use them to wrap things, a kind of jungle saran wrap) and there was this small *mboma* lurking there. He struck at me, and I killed him with my machete."

I let him know I'd like to have a piece, and he was happy to oblige.

Now we had our snake. Louise skinned it, filleted it, and fried it in deep palm fat. Calling witnesses, we ate it as a family. Now, armed with a piece of cooked civet cat given to me by one of the Christian women, I went to the village. Seeking out the *longomo*, I made my case. "Here are my witnesses that my entire family has eaten *mboma*. Now here is a piece of *ebonde* for you to eat." He stared at me, speechless.

At last he spoke. "White man, you may be fool enough to break a white man's taboo, but I am not fool enough to break the black man's."

And that is how we happened to eat snake. By the way, for anyone wondering, the snake looked and tasted a lot like fish.

Evidently the Colossian believers had something of this sort in their background as we read chapter 2:16–23. Living in the world subject to ordinances—"Touch not; taste not; handle not;" which were of no benefit to them who were practicing them.

BREAKING THE TABOOS

Taboo (*tabu*) is a Polynesian word introduced into the English language in the late 18th century by Captain James Cook, a highly skilled and famous English sailor and explorer who visited Tahiti and other Polynesian islands several times on official British business. The word denotes a person, object, or act which is dangerous and therefore forbidden because it is sacred, consecrated, or unclean.

The concept is a familiar one in the Scriptures. Words such as *abomination, defiled, forbidden, unclean,* and so forth occur more than five hundred times in the Old and New Testaments. Historians familiar with ancient languages and religions suggest that the concept of separation from that which is unclean resulted in the coining of the original form of the word "holy". God Himself is the ultimate example of absolute separation from anything which defiles.

But mankind "Professing themselves to be wise...became fools, and changed the glory of the incorruptible God into an image made like to corruptible man, and to birds, and fourfooted beasts and creeping things." (Romans 1:22, 23)

Paul, challenging the Athenians in Acts 17:29, declares: "Forasmuch then as we are the offspring of God, we ought not to think that the Godhead is like unto gold, or silver, or stone, graven by art and man's device."

So mankind in a deadly spiral of darkness and degradation ends up bound in the net of taboo, a reining fear of lurking evil forces that terrorizes them from birth to burial. In Don Richardson's book *Lords of the Earth*, the taboo forbidding any female access to the altars of the gods led a little girl's brothers to fling her into a raging waterfall that plunged into a deep gorge. She had childishly forgotten the taboo and picked flowers in the forbidden area. A study of our own history going back into early Europe and Asia reveals embarrassing darkness in the minds and lives of our ancestors. Even colonial times were rife with taboos and superstitions over which we now shake our heads.

But God!

"If you eat that, you will surely die."

"If you do that, you will be cursed."

How often our people in Congo heard those chilling refrains. Bekanga, Ituku, Ndjoko, and Iyende heard it throughout their childhood years, so they naturally lived by the taboos of their people. When, where, and why such strictures had originated was largely unknown even to the adults. It was simply "the way of the fathers" and thus sacrosanct. For instance, the females were, among other things, forbidden to eat the big black *ngila* monkey. Nor could they eat the black *mbende*. Chicken and eggs were also off limits.

When Bekanga, Ituku, Ndjoko, and Iyende were inducted into the Nkanga Society (remember the story "Becoming a Man"?), they were baptized in a jungle stream. Blindfolded, they listened to the sloshing approach of "something". The Nkanga Society men were shouting "the spirit is coming...the spirit is coming!" Suddenly a stick was thrust between their legs and they were attacked by "the spirit."

Now as baptized members, things became serious. An *ekila* was pronounced, a particular taboo upon which a death oath was required. The *bokanga* fish, a sardine-sized fish found in the jungle streams, was totally off limits. If they ever ate the *bokanga*, certain death would result.

For years these men lived with such taboos. Some were just an inconvenience; others deadly serious. Then, they heard the glorious message of the Gospel and turned to Christ! "If any man be in Christ, he is a new creature: old things are passed away; behold, all things are become new." (II Corinthians 5:17) Immediately the question arose. Could they be real Christians and continue to follow the old ways? Plainly, the answer was no. Even the unsaved still steeped in witchcraft, idolatry, and taboos recognized that. "Prove you are Christians!" was their challenge. "If you are not different, then what these missionaries preach is a lie." *The truth of the Gospel was on the line.* Would the grace of God be appropriated by these new African jungle Christians as the Thessalonian Christians appropriated it, thus showing evidence of being worthy of the kingdom of God? (II Thessalonians 1:4, 5)

In the story "White Man, Do You Eat Snake?" I told you about Bekanga Paul leading the national preachers in swallowing whole the forbidden fish of the Nkanga Society. This challenge to the power of taboos so resonated among the Christians that the breaking of a new believer's most deadly taboo became one of the hallmarks of their faith. Anyone who refused to break a taboo was considered to be nothing more than a professor of faith, not a possessor. This practice resonates of New Testament times. So began the church leadership's

149

custom of investigating the life of each professed Christian who sought baptism. They meet with those to be baptized and question them about their profession of faith, including their taboos. Selecting one of those taboos, the leadership requires each of the believers to stand before the church and eat that which he has believed for all of his life would kill him. It is quite a sight to watch a woman take a boiled egg while standing before the congregation, bow her head in a prayer for courage, and for the first time in her life eat an egg! What a thrill of rejoicing goes through the congregation as the light of freedom shines for the first time upon the face of that new believer.

"If you eat that, you will surely die!" had ruled them for centuries. The occult had held sway since long before the memory of the eldest of them. "If you go there, the evil spirits will get you," they had been told by sorcerers, diviners, and medicine men down throughout their history. Their lives were dyed with physical and spiritual darkness because of it; every facet was dominated by lurking evil. Then arrived the great changing power of God and His Gospel, and liberty became a possibility for the first time in their history.

"If the Son therefore shall make you free, ye shall be free indeed." (John 8:36) We need not fear; God will take care of us. A new day has dawned in the history of a once benighted people. Free indeed! Charles Wesley's hymn says it well:

"Arise, my soul, arise; Shake off thy guilty fears.
The bleeding Sacrifice in my behalf appears:
Before the throne my Surety stands,
My name is written on His hands.

My God is reconciled; His pardoning voice I hear.
He owns me for His child, I can no longer fear.
With confidence I now draw nigh,
And Father, Abba, Father, cry."

A DARK JUNGLE TREK
WITH ETERNAL RESULTS

Mark Grings and I rode the jungle trails together on many occasions, but one of the most memorable trips—and least enjoyable—produced surprising eternal results.

It began when we determined to reach far into the area called the Yalima to the northeast of his station at Yassa. We outfitted ourselves with two bicycles and a metal "chop box" containing a few staple goods such as powdered milk, sugar, salt, cooking oil, a pot for boiling drinking water, a couple pans for preparing meals over an outdoor fire, some enamel plates and cups, safety matches, and a basic first-aid kit. This included, of course, our anti-malarial prophylactic and treatment in case of a malaria attack. A second box contained mosquito nets, bedding, extra clothing, our Lingala Bibles, local currency, .22 caliber ammunition, and our toilet kits. On top of the metal footlockers went two canvas army camp cots, a small kerosene hurricane lantern, and a plastic jug of kerosene. We would hire local villagers along the way to carry the boxes; they would tie them to poles that were shouldered between two men. We would ride our bicycles with machetes slipped through the racks over the back wheels and rifles slung across our shoulders.

Congo trails were just that—foot paths winding through jungle terrain, up and down hills, across swamps, over innumerable stumps, roots, and fallen branches, and through streams spanned by stick bridges. Often these "pig trails" turned into elephant trails on a rainy night due to the deep impressions left by passing elephants, which made it a very rough ride indeed. A kidney experience, you might say.

It was a two-week trip to reach this particular string of villages. We took our Carryall over the first thirty kilometers of dirt road to the government outpost at Dekese, accompanied by my wife and her sister Bessie. They left us at the mouth of the trail and returned to Yassa; we had arranged for them to come back for us on a pre-determined date. From there, Mark and I started out on our bicycles.

Early one afternoon, we approached one of the villages on our itinerary. Each village had a three-room mud and stick guest house reserved for government agents or other white itinerants. We had noticed a trail leading off to the east of the village, so after placing our things in the house, we inquired about where it led. "Are there villages down that trail?"

"Oh yes, three of them," was the response.

"Could we get there and back before dark?" came our second question.

African thought came into play now. Our question was not framed carefully enough to exclude them from giving us the answer they thought we wanted to hear. Sensing that we were hoping those villages would be close enough for a single day's trip, they answered in African fashion, "Yes, you can reach them and return before sundown." In truth, this was impossible and they knew it. However, we received the answer we wanted, so we deserved what we got.

"All right, we'll really make this day count!" we thought. That sounds like real missionaries, doesn't it?

With just our bikes, we struck off down the trail. After a while the path descended into a swamp and we had to carry our bicycles. Nor had we met a single traveler coming our way. By now we should have known we were heading into adventure, but we proceeded until we came to a wide, swift river. The only canoe there was on the other side. Evidently, this was not a frequently traveled trail. We called, hoping someone was over there, but no answer came. Swarms of biting flies had discovered us and were soon creeping into our eyes, inside our ears, down our necks, and into our hair.

"I'll swim across," Mark volunteered, and started making his way upstream along the riverbank. It was a brave idea—but not a very good one. This river could contain any number of creatures which might either object to or welcome his presence. Crocodiles up to sixteen feet long were not uncommon in Congo, and they would welcome a meal. Hippos might well object to this foreigner invading 'their' territory.

But by God's providence, at the moment Mark was ready to dive in, a group of villagers appeared on the other side and crossed with the canoe. We took it then and were soon on the other side, pushing ahead on our bicycles, eventually coming up out of the forest into a plain. Pedaling hard down the winding, sandy path, we finally came to a village. There our Gospel message seemed to fall on deaf ears. Dull eyes void of interest and darkened hearts steeled against the Biblical revelation by their animist upbringing repelled the glorious truth that could have set them free. The same was true of the other two villages further down the trail.

By the time we finished our third evangelistic service, the sun was beginning to glow red on the western horizon. Hurrying back through the plain and down the forest incline to the river, we crossed it just as the sun set and a darkness only found in a jungle wilderness began to surround us. The swamp lay somewhere before us. The trail was now invisible.

Again, as usual, God stepped in. All around us phosphorescent fireflies began to glow a lovely lavender; having absorbed the sun's rays during the day, they now emitted them for our benefit. In that eerie light we began our trek, checking frequently to see if the stars were visible in the dark sky above. Off the trail we would have been unable to see them due to the forest canopy. Out of the swamp now, we reached higher ground.

Suddenly, we were being bitten all over our bodies. Something was invading everywhere—nothing and nowhere was private! We had walked into a marauding horde of *bafumba* (driver ants), the terror of the jungle. Were they coming down the hill or crossing the trail? Only one thing to do—push ahead as quickly as possible, no matter the direction from which they might be coming! And that we did, stumbling and staggering in an effort to get away. We had *bafumba* with their pincers buried in multiple places. But at last the path smoothed, village sounds drifted to us, and the smell of smoke wafted to us as women prepared the evening meal over little wood fires.

At the guest house, we dug out our flashlights and the little kerosene hurricane lamp. For the next hour, we worked to remove the driver ants' pincers from ourselves and each other. A bucket bath was most welcome. Fortunately the bites are not poisonous. Some pincers are so large and strong that, while still attached to the head, they have been used in emergencies to suture wounds.

From village to village we preached, until at last only a long stretch of uninhabited jungle lay between us and the government outpost of Dekese. I had been hampered with a bad case of diarrhea, but despite this, I was headed home. At such times, the nationals would say I had a wind blowing at my back which made it difficult for them to keep up with me, well or sick. And so it was that day. I will not bore you with accounts of my side trips off the trail. At last I came to the foot of the long hill which led to Dekese, where Louise and Bessie waited in the Carryall.

It was a hot afternoon. I was exhausted, and there was no way I could push my bicycle up that seemingly endless hill. Leaning it against a tree where I knew someone would pick it up, I began the ascent on foot. I walked a while...crawled a while...walked again...and crawled again. Weeping on occasion out of sheer weakness, I finally cleared the top of the hill and the Carryall was there! You can be sure that never did a young man sleep with such comfort and contentment in the arms of his beloved as I did that night with my Louise.

But that is not the end of the story. Years later, after Congo had been torn by the ruthless Simba revolution which burned our churches and schools and murdered our pastors and Christians, we were again at Yassa with Mark and other family members. A group of twelve men appeared at the back of the lawn near Pastor Booto Bankese's house. Mark and I, curious, walked over to them.

"Do you know us?" they asked.

"No, you don't look familiar," we replied.

"Do you remember when, late in the day, you arrived at three villages and preached to people who wanted to hear nothing you were telling them? And how you left late in the evening and were certainly caught in darkness by the time you reached the river? Well, as a result of your preaching, we eventually came to Christ. Now we are

157

preachers of the Gospel, and come here for training with Pastor Booto Bankese!"

Did we remember! How could we ever forget? Could our memories fail to recall that eventful day? How we rejoiced in the marvelous grace of the God of Heaven, Who in His sovereignty arranged an adventurous jungle trek with such glorious eternal results. A very evident case of Psalms 32:8:

"I will instruct thee and teach thee in the way thou shalt go: I will guide thee with Mine eye."

STONED AT KANGALA

Mark Grings and I were on a village trip to the west of our station at Nkole Nkema. We drove over the winding, muddy, hilly jungle terrain, stopping in villages along the way to hold open air evangelistic meetings and encourage the believers.

Exiting the jungle, we continued the drive across the rolling grassy plains. Now the road was sandy and we were able to move along at a faster clip, though never over forty miles an hour because of the truism that every good stretch ended with a bad one.

We pulled into Kangala. This village was influenced by a Roman Catholic presence, and we could expect some opposition. Still as steeped in animistic heathenism as villages untouched by any church, this village merely had added the element of syncretism. That is, their animistic ways and superstitions had been well mixed with Catholic dogma. In such places, our presence and preaching were not very propitious.

On this particular day, the young men were especially offensive, which we ignored. But as we started to drive out of the village, they ran behind us. Suddenly stones and sticks began to fly, whacking into the car, evidently upon the instructions of the itinerant priest.

159

Stopping the car, I jumped out of the vehicle and grabbed one of the young men, intending to take him to a government official to report this illegal activity. Putting an arm lock on him, I walked him toward the car. My evident knowledge of elemental Judo held the others off, but an uncle arrived with a machete with which he made a swipe across my left wrist, freeing the young man. With that, the whole gang ran pell-mell away from us. The cut was minor.

News in Africa travels very quickly, almost as if carried on the wind. When word of the incident reached the paramount chief of the district, he made a trip to Kangala. Word of his impending arrival emptied the village as the people disappeared into the nearby forest. So he set up camp in the village rest house along with his retinue to outwait them. Once they returned, he let them know he would not countenance a repeat of the illegal attack upon the missionaries, and that severe punishment would be meted out if it happened again.

While such physical action is uncommon on the mission field, there are certain social circumstances in which they expect it and respect the manhood of the persons involved. In forty-four years on the mission fields of Africa and South America, I have experienced few such incidents.

A second occurred while on a bicycle trek; I encountered two young men beating a feeble old man. Putting those two on the ground and standing between them and the old man, I was able with God's help to protect him and enforce rational action on their part. A third occurred in another Catholic-influenced village, but the circumstances there were different so I departed the scene without seeking redress. Matthew 5:10–12 gives us a Scriptural perspective; "Blessed are they which are persecuted for righteousness' sake: for theirs is the kingdom of heaven."

Our ministry in the land of Suriname, South America began in 1965 after we were evacuated from Congo, and we entered a field where adverse situations had caused three missionary couples to leave. Our ministry was with the Bush Negroes of Suriname, famous for the fifty-year-long guerrilla war they fought with the Dutch government beginning at about the time of the American Civil War. They won that bloody war and became a nation within a nation. Thus, they looked down on the white man as inferior. This was soon evident once we settled at the station near the village of Ricanau Moffo on the Cottica River. One of the things in my favor was the fact that I could out-lift any one of the men. Of course, I had done some work on bar bells, and I was extremely fit from our rugged life in Africa. By the grace of God, this together with a number of miraculous demonstrations of God's power established our acceptability to live among them.

THE MOTOR WOULDN'T RUN

Throughout the years we served in Congo, we had only been able to get to the westernmost villages of our large outreach area a disappointingly few times. The logistics of vehicle, boat, and bicycle travel taxed all the resources of our physical strength, money, and time. Now determined to get to those distant villages, Mark Grings and I left our vehicle and mounted our bicycles to reach the banks of the Lukenie River. This river flows westward until it empties into the great Kasai River within a short distance of the Kasai's conjunction with the monster Congo, second in the world only to Brazil's Amazon River. Bordered by towering, tangled jungle on both sides, the Lukenie flows deep and black, forming the entire northern border of the area God gave us to reach in the heart of Congo. Home of giant crocodiles and huge hippopotamuses, it is a river in which we baptized with caution!

Our intent on this trip was to use the Lukenie as a conveyance to cut hours and miles off what a bicycle trip would take. We had been told a government boat was tied up across the river and hoping to leave soon. Once we had arrived at the water, they confirmed their willingness to take us along as passengers on the deep, heavy, metal boat. We boarded with our bicycles and gear.

The starter growled, and the engine spun, coughed, and died. Further attempts to start it were unsuccessful, so Mark and I helped remove the fuel lines to get at the fuel starvation problem. Sure enough, poor maintenance had allowed rust and other debris to clog the line at the point it entered the carburetor. Once the lines were cleared, we thought we would soon be on our way.

Alas, another problem confronted us. We'd been able to tap the fuel line nuts loose enough to disassemble and clear the line, but there was no wrench to tighten the nuts well enough to prevent gasoline from spraying over the engine. This was before the days of Leather-man pocket tools, so we were forced to continue our trip by paddle rather than engine.

Pushing off into the main current, we began to drift down the river. Hours passed and darkness settled across the jungle. Once in a while the sternman of the boat put a few strokes into the water to keep us well aligned in the current. Night birds called, an occasional hippo was disturbed by our passing, and fish swirled and splashed. About midnight, lights appeared on the bend far ahead. Our destination was in sight. But what was the cause of the grunting and roaring going on? Hippos holding some kind of a convention were making a threatening commotion. In a canoe we would have been more concerned, but even our boat was vulnerable. My .30-06 was cocked and loaded, just in case. Quite a show!

Once ashore, we found a place to stay the night. Services in several locations followed as we began working our way back upriver, but now by jungle trail, riding our bicycles where we could and walking other stretches. Finally, we had about thirty miles left to cover to reach the last village. Mark and I had learned that chocolate bars were good energy sources, and we were munching as we went. The area was alive with game. At last we came to a swampy area, indicating that a river was near—the final obstacle before the last village. It was dark as the Lukenie and swift as it rushed to join the mother river. The only bridge across the challenging divide was a tree trunk with a vine to grasp tied above it.

Can you picture the two of us attempting to cross with cycles over our shoulders? Our canvas shoes held their grip; our balance, though sometimes precarious, was maintained. Step by careful step we advanced, glad there were no disruptions. One more step—made it! We breathed a sigh of relief, smiled in congratulations, and thanked the Lord for a safe crossing. We had done as the Lord commanded: "Go out into the highways and hedges...that my house may be filled." (Luke 14:23)

And so ended another journey carrying the Gospel to a people living in darkness. David's prayer in Psalm 27:11 was answered for us: "Teach me Thy way, O Lord, and lead me in a plain path..."

CAPE BUFFALO

The African Cape Buffalo is big[1], strong, and cunning. Some say he is the most dangerous animal in Africa, and I tend to agree. So when tribal folks asked me to rid their area of a particularly troublesome bull, I made a mental note to make sure to do the job right. On a previous occasion, I had warned a Belgian territorial agent *not* to shout "I got him!" and run toward a buffalo he had downed. He didn't listen! After he shot the animal and started running towards it, the fatally wounded bull rose from the ground and charged the man, who turned and fled. The buffalo butted the agent in the middle of his back, sending him flying into an unconscious heap. The bull then rooted his nose under the man, intending to throw him into the air and catch him on his horns. At that moment the bull breathed his last and crumpled to the ground. The fortunate Belgian official awoke to find himself lying back to back with more than a thousand pounds of buffalo.

Yes, I would face the bull if he came in sight, but carefully. Mark Grings and I had traveled about one hundred fifty miles on this particular narrow dirt road, preaching the Gospel in a number of villages

---

1   It took sixteen strong men to lift one, gutted and laid on a rack

along the way and counseling our national pastors. Arriving at the village of Dika late in the afternoon, we gathered the people together in the church for an evening service before spending the night in the guest house.

The guest house was a large mud and stick house with a thatch roof and dirt floors. As usual, we swept the floor with a twig broom to get rid of goat droppings and fleas that might well be there. Then we set up our canvas cots and tied two 1-inch thick poles, perhaps six feet long, to each end of our cots. To these we tied our mosquito nets. The prevalence of malaria did not encourage us to sleep without them. Spiders, centipedes, scorpions, and snakes were another incentive for keeping ourselves well-netted during the night. However, our nets did not keep out the goat fleas which on occasion tortured me in the dark, leaving welts that caused bothersome itching. A light sheet, thin blanket, small pillow, and the ever-present flashlight completed our beds. Our .22 caliber rifles stood propped against the nearest net poles. We couldn't be sure the dropped-down reed shutter which served as a door would keep out night prowlers, and we wanted to be prepared in case they nosed in on us.

We left for the buffalo hunt before dawn the next morning, taking several village men with us. Dika is nestled near the Lukenie River. Buffalo roamed the plains and *bipoka* (groves of trees) dotted the area across the river and through the jungle. Viewed from the air, this area would present a large sweep of grasslands scattered with groves several acres in size. This is the African Cape buffalo's favorite kind of place. Moving along the dark path in single file we kept a sharp ear out for any hippos or elephants which might be in the cassava fields. We were not anxious to encounter these beasts in the dark, but could tackle them if necessary.

Soon we stood on the bank of the Lukenie River. On other occasions we had come upon hippos cavorting and contesting here, roaring and plunging in the water. These massive beasts can measure up to five feet tall and fifteen feet long, can weigh up to four tons, and are armed with giant lower canine teeth (up to two feet long) and incisors longer than fourteen inches. When these monsters are in a bad mood, they are not to be trifled with. On this particular morning, however, the water was quiet and we proceeded to enter our dugout canoes and paddle silently across the river.

The sky was beginning to change from black to gray as we moved toward the grasslands. Picking our way along the forest path, our feet became wet with the early morning dew. Dawn found us at the edge of the grasslands, the low fog lifting to reveal groves scattered here and there, a beautiful full-color mosaic of dark trees and light green grass as the sun made its appearance low in the eastern sky. In single file we began moving across the plain, all the while keeping a sharp lookout in every direction, scanning to and fro for the telltale flash of black or reddish brown that would signal the presence of buffalo.

Then we spotted them hundreds of yards away, a small herd of perhaps twelve to fourteen. There was a mixture of big black bulls and smaller brown males and females. "Keep low," we hissed to each other, for buffalo are keen of sight and smell; not easy to approach. Putting a grove of trees between us and them, we hoped to cut off our scent from drifting their way as we worked our way toward them.

Tight against the grove we crept, then entered it and worked to its outside edge facing the unaware herd. There they were—what a beautiful sight! Majestic, proud, and powerful; they were delicious, nutritious food for our family and national Christians in this jungle mission field where no beef was raised.

Crack! Spoke a hunter's gun. His quarry staggered then began to run. *Crack! Crack! Crack!* The sound of his shot echoed off the groves behind and around us. The herd scattered, unsure where to go, and a big bull thundered past crossing left to right. *Makalele Monene* tracked him, thundered, and he fell. Our family and many others would eat well, thank God.

But we had a problem. The other wounded bull had entered another stand of trees. We decided he must be tracked, but as these animals are extremely dangerous when wounded, that was a risky proposition indeed. He had entered the dark environs of a thick grove. Brave was the man who volunteered to enter that grove in his pursuit—but also smart, for he could track it while climbing from tree to tree in that dense forest. The cunning beast would be lying in wait for the fool that would attempt to come after him on the ground.

Calling to us, the tracker reported but little blood. Then came an excited yell, "*L-o-o-k-o-t-o!* There he is. Aigh! He's after me but he can't reach me up this tree. It's only a flesh wound, nothing for him to worry about."

Giving up the assault, the buffalo moved off through the grove to eventually regroup with the others who had scattered. Our brave fellow descended the tree and exited the grove to a round of applause.

Butchering began next. We missionaries have become experts at dressing animals large and small, producing various cuts for numerous purposes. But here in the field, only the main sections were separated for carrying. In fact, runners were sent back to the village for help. With one front leg tied on a pole, a national and I started off towards Dika. Mark stayed behind with the other men making manageable loads from that big bull. I, of course, was still carrying *Makalele Monene*, and the national with me had his spear.

Something large and dark appeared on the edge of the wide plain, right up against the jungle. My eyes, accustomed to the hunt and never resting, spotted this change immediately. An elephant? The shadow was not large enough for that.

"Look there," I said to my companion. "Over there against the forest—three, four hundred yards away." His sharp eyes now focused on the object. "Buffalo," he said. "It looks like the big, bad one that has troubled folks passing this way."

"Well," I thought, "Now we meet."

His head came up, his sharp vision trained on us. Something rose up in him, something saying *"Get them!"* I do not pretend to understand it; I only report it. The buffalo made his decision and swung around, not toward the jungle and safety, but toward us and war. Amazed, I watched him head straight at us, swiftly covering a hundred yards. Lifting *Makalele Monene*, I sighted and squeezed the trigger. At that distance we could hear the bullet thwack into him. He staggered but came on, now limping on his right front leg. *Makalele Monene* spoke again, and again the bullet found its mark, but he kept coming. Hunters of big game know that the secret is putting the first bullet in the right place. A large animal aroused by wounding will sometimes become impervious to anything that follows.

And so it was with this malevolent beast. Staggering but refusing to go down until we met face to face, he plunged toward us. At last we stood fifty feet apart, he pawing with the wounded leg, blowing with the exertion, and snorting his coming attack. What a scene! It would be hard to imagine anything more compelling. I was ready, but unsure what to do. My last cartridge was in the chamber, and he had withstood others over a four hundred yard charge. I had not missed; the shots were well placed. He should have been down—but he was not.

"Would one of those *bongondo* trees (like a scrub oak) hold us if we climbed up?" I asked my fellow hunter.

"That depends on how well you could hold on when he slams that huge body into the tree," He replied. Was there a grin on his face in spite of the circumstances...?

Suddenly, the buffalo collapsed sideways to us, with his head half turned as he looked at us with one baleful eye. Thus we faced each other, me standing fifty feet away and that majestic bull still determined to get me but now without the strength. One cartridge remained in my gun and none in my pocket. I concluded that a head shot was the only thing that would mercifully end this standoff. My target was right through the temple, just under that massive plate of bone from which issued the sweeping, deadly curved horns. Taking into account that at this distance my scope would cause the gun to shoot a little high, I held it an inch or so low. Alas, given the strain of my body, the shot was still just a little high. Slamming into the bone plate it twisted his head, and the buffalo stood up! Now the fat was indeed in the fire.

We heard Mark running toward us, calling. "I heard a shot and thought you had spotted an antelope. But when other shots followed, I decided it was an elephant, and tried to get here as fast as I could."

"A cartridge," I requested.

"Take two," was the reply.

This shot went through the heart, and the buffalo broke, racing away towards the safety of the forest now much too far away. His legs began to wobble, the knees went bowlegged—and then he was down and dead.

Upon butchering him we found his heart punctured by several

holes, any one of which should have been fatal except for the power of his purpose which sent him charging our way.

Would you find it believable if I said there was respect between us in those last moments?

"Dumb animal," you say. But I see him as an animal dangerous and mean, but with great character. Each of us in our own right and armed with our own weapons had dueled to a conclusion. Someone had to win. He had often won; a powerful, dominating beast he had been in his own kingdom. He lost, still full of fire. I won, with a mixture of sorrow for his death and admiration for his incredible bravery. *What an animal!*

Thoughts turn to God's original order in Genesis 1:28 of the dominion of man over "every living thing that moveth upon the earth," the restatement in 9:2 after the flood, and then in the beautiful extolling of God's name in Psalm 8. Here it points out that God "made [man] to have dominion over the works of [His] hands... and put all things under his feet." He's deserving of praise, Him Whose name is "excellent in all the earth."

AT DEATH'S DOOR:
A VERY CLOSE CALL

The mission station of Yassa is located in one of several scattered grassy plains. These create a mosaic of verdant grasslands interspersed with dark green jungle groves until, at last, nothing but the massive trees and thick underbrush of the great Congo jungle stretches as far as the eye can see. Cape buffalo, bush bucks, goat antelope, anteaters, jackals, civet cats, bustards, guinea fowl, partridges, and quail share the expanse, as well as snakes, both poisonous and harmless. Many varieties of antelope, from the Chihuahua-sized dik-dik to the horse-sized *mbuji*, inhabit the jungle along with wild boars, monkeys, chimpanzees, apes, gorillas, elephants, huge pythons, scores of other snakes, and numerous varieties of jungle birds. This is the fabled African jungle, a place of great beauty, relentless pursuit and capture, satisfied passions, and breathless escapes. Yet more importantly, it is a place of ancient cultures and darkness of mind and spirit, of young beauty and ravaged old age, of long-controlling customs and short-lived people.

Just a short walk from the jungle, Yassa sits backed up against a large grove for shelter from the formidable winds which at times tear the thatch roofs off village huts. For years, this village has been the only Gospel beacon to a number of other villages in that area, both on the plains and in the jungle. Mark Grings and I had been planning a month-long assault on the Satanic darkness that binds the villages spread along trails shadowed by the great forest canopy. Our feet and bicycles were familiar with the winding paths that lay before us, and we knew we would find in the villages mud and stick houses in which to sleep. Rather than leave Louise (Mark's sister) and our children alone on our isolated station at Nkole Nkema, we had arranged for them to be with longtime missionary friends, the Browers, at their station.

Stopping along the way to Yassa, we dropped in at a mission station which had a doctor and a clinic. Mark wasn't feeling well, and we hoped to find some medication. Little did we realize that within a couple of days Mark would be back there for emergency surgery!

A long drive over sandy roads in the plains brought us to the Lodi River. Wending our way down the winding road, we were happy to find the ferry on our side. Boarding the ferry is a little tricky since the heavy planks which serve as a ramp have to be lifted and lined up with the wheels of the vehicle. One of the men motioned us up onto the ferry. Then the planks were lifted off and dropped at the water's edge. The ferry engine started with difficulty. The battery was low and the engine sounded as if it had other problems as well, a circumstance that would come back to haunt us. We swung out into the current and angled our way across the river, repeated the boarding process, and then descended the planks to solid ground.

After the climb up away from the river, we worked our way along the rough jungle road and broke out into the plain, passing a beautiful little lake nestled in a cliff-surrounded hollow on our left. Going through Yassa, we scattered goats and chickens before us, the only other traffic on the seldom traveled road. We swung off to the left through some trees and arrived at our Yassa station. Mark took medicine for his continued pain and we retired for the night, expecting to complete our preparations the next day for the long bicycle trip.

Morning dawned on a still very uncomfortable coworker. As old-fashioned missionaries, more often than not one would ignore physical pain as a bother, determined to get the task done. So the day progressed as we packed our chop box with food staples, readied our army camp cots, and checked our list of necessary items to take on this trip. By this time Mark was sweating and an unhealthy pallor clouded his face. This wasn't the usual case of upset stomach. It was time to get into the Chevy Carryall and make our way another couple of hours through the jungle to the government doctor at Dekese. A suspicion crossed our minds that the problem would be diagnosed as appendicitis.

The Dekese doctor confirmed our suspicions and told us surgery would be necessary.

"I'm sorry," he said, "but there is no way I can attempt it without another doctor in attendance. I suggest we take Mark in your vehicle back across the Lodi River to the government center, where another doctor can assist."

So we loaded Mark into the Carryall, removing seats to accommodate a cot for him. Driving carefully over the rough road, we worked our way slowly out of the forest into the plains. There, we could slightly increase our speed, but we slowed again as we entered the groves located in the deep valleys. Finally, we started the descent to the river. Another turn, one last steep drop, and we moved into view of the ferry landing. Alas, the ferry was on the other side. Worse—the ferry was broken down and would not run again that day. The doctor found a national to take him across in a dugout canoe. But the doctor was not at the station, and the only vehicle on the other side, a Volkswagen Bug, was completely unsuitable for transporting our appendicitis sufferer. Discouraged, the doctor returned to our side of the river.

Only one option was left to us: return to Dekese and radio a missionary doctor for a small plane flight the next morning. You can only imagine the pain the return trip caused Mark as we retraced our way as carefully and gently as possible over those miles of rough road. Hours later we pulled in to the doctor's house at Dekese. We made short-wave radio contact with Dr. Poole, and he agreed to come as early as possible the next morning. Graciously, the doctor and his wife gave up their bed for Mark. Panting in pain, sleep would not come. I spent the hours of the night calling upon the God of Heaven for intervention on Mark's behalf. At some point early in the morning, Mark's pain suddenly faded. Unless God had worked a miraculous cure, that could only mean the appendix had burst. Now widespread infection, peritonitis, was a real danger.

It seemed the dawn would never come, but at last the glow of day appeared on the horizon. A heavy fog lay on the land. Slowly the emerging orb established its rulership of the day, and the fog began to lift. Then the buzz of a small, single engine plane could be heard. Dr. Poole had not been able to fly his plane for a couple of weeks, due to these very heavy morning mists. We witnessed a miracle as the Lord's hand brushed them aside, just as He had bid the boisterous winds to be still long ago. There he was, banking around across town and back toward the grass landing strip. We bundled Mark into the vehicle once again and proceeded to the airstrip. Soon Mark was lying in the plane, the government doctor boarded, and the pilot, Dr. Poole, took his place. Engine at take-off pitch, the little plane swung around and soon lifted into the sky. "There he goes," I murmured. "God watch over you, Mark."

The next task was to get a telegram off to Louise with the news of Mark's illness and the destination to which he was being taken. There was no telephone at the mission station of Kifwanzondo (the Browers' station), or virtually any other mission station at that stage in Congo's history; a telegram was our only hope of making contact. The nearest place to Kifwanzondo capable of receiving a telegram was Idiofa, about twenty kilometers (approx. 12 ½ miles) away. The telegram sent, I returned to the car and started back down the long stretch of road over which I had already driven three times in the last two days. With no Mark to require slower speeds and more care in the frequent rough spots, I pushed my speed in hopes of finding the ferry operating again. About four hours later the ferry came into view, coming across the river! Thank the Lord, there was room on the return trip (a couple of big freight trucks could easily have loaded it to capacity and blocked my passage), and the crossing went smoothly. I urged the vehicle up the hill on the other side, through the stretches of jungle, and at last into the plains—racing toward Bulape, the mission hospital, and Mark.

In the meantime, the telegram had been received at Idiofa and was waiting at the post office. Louise, unaware that her brother's life hung in the balance, was at Kifwanzondo. But God had another bearer of news come to the post office that morning. Brother Jantz, a fellow missionary and friend of the Browers, was told of the telegram and picked it up for Louise. It was a miracle in itself that he knew where she was. Soon a vehicle containing Mark's brother Bob and his wife, Winifred, with Louise and our three children, was on the road for the slow, two-hundred-mile journey to Bulape.

I pulled in under a full head of steam sometime in the afternoon. To my relief and to the praise of the Lord I heard that Mark had come through surgery successfully and was resting well. Peritonitis had indeed set in, the infection was badly spread, and the burst appendix was extremely inflamed. Given the length of time the infection had to develop, Dr. Poole concluded that Mark's excellent physical condition and the intervention of the God of Heaven had been all that could have pulled him through. Many hours later, the family arrived to find him resting comfortably in the mission guest house and able to eat the nourishing custard made by Mrs. Poole. The Pooles gave the whole of their lives in Congo to the service of their Savior. Un-numbered Africans and many missionaries rose up to call them blessed, and we were among them. Many years later, Mark, now married, was at Bulape with his wife, Wyla, for the birth of their daughter, Esther Joy—and the Pooles were still there to assist.

A very close call, indeed, at death's door. "But God, who is rich in mercy, for His great love wherewith He loved us," has given us a glorious promise which He, of course, shows Himself faithful to keep. (Ephesians 2:4)

"Call unto Me, and I will answer thee, and shew thee great and mighty things, which thou knowest not." (Jeremiah 33:3) We called; naturally, He answered.

A CASE OF POLYGAMY

Mark Grings and I were ascending from the valley of the Lodi River in our Jeep station wagon. Its four-wheel drive traction and rugged suspension showed its breeding on the dirt road replete with washed out gullies, fallen branches, and muddy hills. The air was hot and humid and we drove with our windows down. All the better also to hear the sounds of the jungle around us, alerting us to the presence of game birds and monkeys— one of the main staples of our national workers' diets. "Bringing home the bacon" did not hurt our reputation with the nationals.

On many occasions, folks in the villages near the road would seek to hitch a ride with the infrequent vehicles which ventured into this area. So we were not surprised when we were flagged down at one of them, albeit the flagging seemed more urgent than usual.

"Oh, please help us!" they cried. "We have a dead body to take to the next village (some miles ahead) to be buried, and it is so far to carry her." A dead body? Why not? We've carried almost everything else in our vehicles. Without a lot of consultation between us, Mark and I agreed. "Malamu, tokokumba yango (That's fine, we will carry it)," we answered.

181

Bad mistake. This woman was several days dead and we could smell the blanket-wrapped bundle before it reached our vehicle. Helping to carry the body was a young woman with tears streaming down her face. A younger sister, we wondered?

It turned out she was younger, but not a sister. She was the second wife of the same husband! The body fit in the space between the seat behind us and the back door. The smell filtered into every nook and cranny of the vehicle and every particle of our breath. Any missionary working with tribal peoples becomes familiar with the smell of death and long overdue burials, but this was the worst I had experienced up to that time. Our gag reflex was on constant alert as I drove with my head out the window on my side and Mark with his head out on the other.

The astonishing thing, however, was the fact that the younger wife was cradling the corpse in her arms and weeping out her heartbroken loss. Now, as missionaries we understood that a display of anguished emotion over someone's death was expected—necessary, in fact, because of the fear of retribution from the dead upon the living who did not show sufficient sorrow over an individual's death. Rolling on the ground, filthy with dirt and ashes, clothing absent or in disarray, screams of agony—all this could be expected of anyone with any connection to the deceased. But there was another note in this wailing, a note of love: the love of a younger sister for her beloved older sister.

How could this be? Why wasn't the younger woman happy to see the older out of the way? Such questions evince a lack of understanding of African life. Let me see if I can give you a little insight into the reality of tribal Africa.

It might begin with a wife speaking to her husband. "You're not much of a man, are you?"

"What did you say?"

"I said that you're not much of a man."

"Now why would you say something like that?"

"Because a real man would have had a second wife by this time."

"A second wife?"

"Yes, a second wife. I'm tired of doing all the work. I plant and harvest the garden, do the fishing, cook all the meals, and take care of this gang of children. It is time I had help."

"Oh, you want help, do you?"

"Yes, I want help; I have already chosen the one to do it."

"Who is that?"

"The beautiful young girl, Mboko's daughter, who lives at the other end of the village."

"Her? Why, her father will want a fortune for a girl like that. I admit I've been saving *nkonga*[1] for such a purpose, but..."

"Oh come on, you're a rich man. Certainly you can afford the bride price for another wife."

"All right, I'll send my brother to talk to her family about it." (A man would never go in person, fearing the shame of being turned down.)

So the two families meet, a price is agreed upon to reimburse the family for raising the bride, incidentally supplying the bride price for one of that father's sons. A slim, striking young woman comes to live with the husband as his second wife. He builds a mud and stick house for her with a smaller cooking shed and she moves into his little community. With two wives to care for, he commutes from one house

---

1   Copper bars made from pouring melted copper into a form in the soil.

to the other, giving each wife a week at a time. If the first wife has chosen well, the second may indeed become a companion to her, and upon the older wife's death she may truly mourn her passing.

"My sister, my sister. How will I live without you? My sister, my sister."

So it was that Mark and I drove off with this incredible scene playing out behind us—a case of ancient African polygamy.

"Inasmuch as ye have done it unto one of the least of these my brethren, ye have done it unto me." (Matthew 25:40b)

COBRA IN THE LIVING ROOM

*"Fear thou not; for I am with thee: be
not dismayed; for I am thy God: I will
strengthen thee; yea, I will help thee; yea,
I will uphold thee with the right hand
of my righteousness."*
(Isaiah 41:10)

We stood in front of our little mud and stick house, feeling
the intense heat of the old "rats nest" going up in a fountain of flame
and mourning a little for the loss. It had been the home into which
we had taken little David at a year and a half old, and then Jonathan
and Deborah as tiny, newborn infants. But it was eventually eaten out
by termites and now groaned in preparation for collapse. The structure was dangerous and its day was past; the flames were a sad but
merciful end.

Our new cement block house was now finished at last. Well,
almost finished. We were still using the pit latrine out back, but there
was a bathroom with a big galvanized tub and a sealed hole where a
toilet might one day stand. And there was a corrugated galvanized roof
for catching clean water during the big rain storms that had turned
the thatch roofing of our old house on end so that the rain poured
through unhindered. The new windows were covered with screens (no

185

more having the house filled with malaria-bearing mosquitoes) and we actually had wooden doors which could close, making it more difficult for snakes, tarantulas, scorpions, and centipedes to enter. After living for more than five years in our mud and stick "jungle rats' nest" with doors and windows covered only with raffia palm shutters, this house looked and felt like a palace. The five thousand cement blocks for its construction had been handmade with the help of our school children and Bible Institute students, who had laboriously carried sand and water up from a jungle stream.

The floor of the house was cement, albeit very thin, which I had troweled smooth. No more reed mats on a dirt floor with termites by the trillion rattling against our passing on their rooftop. The living room-dining room combination was convenient. A cement block lamp stand head high against one wall marked the separation. That was where our Coleman pressure lamp stood (we had no electricity, of course), along with our little Philips short-wave radio which operated off a separate six-volt battery. (There were no transistor radios in those days.) The ceiling was plywood painted white, above which we stored supplies in the space between it and the roofing. A steep ironwood staircase in the hallway gave us access. "It is strong enough to carry an elephant's weight," I thought, after drilling the nail holes and dipping the large nails in motor oil in order to drive them in.

There were three bedrooms and a 6' x 10' office, my province. An in-house kitchen would have made the dwelling both hot and dirty with the heat and smoke from our wood stove, so instead, a two-room kitchen stood just outside the back door, attached by a walkway. Here was Louise's domain. A storeroom with shelves for canned local fruits, juices, and meats adjoined the cooking area with its homemade cupboards and work counter covered with a laboriously flattened sheet of galvanized roofing metal. On the opposite side was the big black iron wood-burning stove with its hot water tank. It was the kind of stove common in old-time farm houses. There was no running water, but barrels of rain water filled from the roof during the eight-month rainy season stood just outside. During the four months when the heavens went dry, water was carried in buckets from a jungle spring a mile away to keep us supplied.

This was our home, set with its back to the jungle and its face to the sweep of our lawn and the broad expanse of African grasslands bordered by more jungle on the horizon.

One day as I passed the entrance to the living room, a quick movement caught my eye. Stepping into the room I could see several feet of dark-bodied snake gliding under a triangular dish cupboard we had constructed especially to fit into the far corner of our new dining area. In that cupboard were our wedding dishes.

"Well now, what kind of creature is that?" I wondered. Crouching down at a safe distance, I peered under the cupboard and was not exactly pleased to discover a cobra. Can you imagine? This cobra had entered our new abode without so much as an "If you please?". Now one thing you do not want to do when you find such a reptile in your house is to leave the room to go for a weapon. You may well return to find it has gone elsewhere, and you know not where! Not a pleasant thought.

So the thing to do is have someone else get one. I yelled, "Louise, we have a cobra in the living room. Bring me a straight stick about five feet long and 'so thick!'" Well, missionary wives whose houses are invaded by cobras tend to be very cooperative when asked for a stick five feet long and "so thick". Now the first problem was to remove the tables and chairs so the battlefield was clear.

Next, "How do we get that snake out from under the dish cupboard?"

"Shoot it," you say.

"No, where would the bullet go after it had gone through the snake? Off the wall, through the cupboard (endangering the precious wedding dishes), or rattling around the room? No, a gun will not do."

"Well, what about a machete then?"

"Nope. Too short. It has to be a stick about five feet long and 'so thick.'"

I thought if I poked it and made it angry—I mean, really upset—it would come out, lift its head in its typical pre-strike stance, and spread its hood. At that point it should look pretty much like a baseball sitting on a batting tee, and then it would be playing my game: baseball. So I carefully began poking, and it started hissing its displeasure.

Poke, poke.

Hiss, hiss.

Poke, poke.

Hiss, hiss, HISS.

And then out he came, rose up nicely, and posed with hood spread. Whack! Home run! Score: one dead cobra. Oh well, maybe it was too much to expect our nice new house to be 'snake-proof'.

My wife Louise has often said, "Safety lies, not in the absence of danger, but in the presence of God." We have found that to be true over and over again during our more than fifty years in the jungles of Africa and South America, as this story illustrates. And doesn't Psalm 91:13 tell us "Thou shalt tread upon...the adder...and trample under feet" these objects of fear and danger?

KILLING A POISONOUS SNAKE A MISSIONARY WIFE'S WAY

"Thou shalt tread upon the lion and the adder: the young lion and the dragon shalt thou trample under feet."
(Psalm 91:13)

Are you afraid of snakes, especially the poisonous variety? My wife grew up in the wilds of Congo, and she was. You would have been too, had the houses in which you slept been built of bark or mud and sticks, with thatch roofs, dirt floors, and no windows or doors that could keep such serpents out. It was one thing to have hyenas laugh and howl just yards from your house, and leopards prowl the woods in which your girlhood house stood. But snakes indoors—those were something else entirely. Her mother wasn't there, having gone to be with the Lord when Louise was eight. So there was no soft motherly embrace in which to snuggle for comfort, reassurance, and safety.

It did not help to see snakes either, especially the day there was a thick-bodied viper coiled, deadly dangerous, just off the steep trail leading down to their natural spring water hole at the base of the cliff. It was a good thing her brother had seen it before it launched its deadly fangs! Nights were especially frightening. She could imagine one of those menaces slipping into the house, its tongue flicking, the heat-sensing pits in its head straining to detect warm blood within striking distance. In her dreams she felt rather than saw the snake as it twined around the ceiling support pole and ascended toward her bed upstairs. With a start she would awaken, clammy and cold.

Was it any wonder then, when she walked into our 'jungle rat's nest' of a house, that a twinge of apprehension went through her for her little son David? That fear had to be dealt with, for his sake and the children to follow. There was a God in heaven, and she knew that God and His Word. At the age of eight she had already read her Bible from cover to cover, and has read it many more times since. Chapters and whole books were recorded verse by verse in her excellent, retentive memory. They came flowing out in perfect order during those times when, with great pleasure, she meditated upon God and His Word.

And so it was to God and His word that she went for freedom from the fear of snakes. "Call upon me, and I will answer thee, and shew thee great and mighty things, which thou knowest not," the God of Heaven had spoken to Jeremiah, and now He spoke to her. She called and He kept his promise; the fear of snakes left her. Her children would have a mother who knew how to get into the presence of God and could also lead them there. The victory was hers.

One of the proofs of the victory is the subject of this story. We moved out of the old mud and stick house after five years and built a cement block house. It was in our new house that Louise met "her" snake face to face. I was out hunting, an event which took place about every two weeks when the meat stored in our little kerosene refrigerator was about used up. The plains around us would usually yield a small *nse* antelope or on rarer occasions the big *nkai* bush buck. We took what we could keep in the small freezing unit and then supplied

190

our boarding school boys with the rest. A couple of hours in the late afternoon would suffice for the hunt. Louise would hear the bark of *Makalele Monene* and know we would soon be skinning and dressing our new meat supply, and there would be liver for supper.

But that evening something very unusual happened: visitors arrived! Being so far off the beaten track, that was a rare occasion indeed; it took more effort than most potential guests would put out to find us on our side of the Kasai River. In this case, however, one of the visitors knew Winifred Ferrel Grings, my wife's sister-in-law, so here they were. They had ferried across the two-mile-wide river on a small ferry boat, strained their way up the steep bank, and followed a rough dirt road that ascended through the jungle to the plains and on to the village of Nkole Nkema and our house. Even though we had no idea of their coming, they knew that they could count on our delighted welcome and old-fashioned missionary hospitality. Company in our isolated situation was always stimulating. What good fellowship we would have sharing what God was doing in our separate fields!

Now, Louise had come face to face with a big black snake, an unwanted intruder of dark satin coils, when she drew back the curtain on the old crate that served as a cupboard in the kitchen-shed. There it was in all its sinister glory on the second shelf next to some pots and pans. Iyende, her kitchen helper, took care of that one. That black snake was pretty bold to stare Louise straight in the eye, but he paid for it. Once while eating lunch, I had shot a ten-foot-long viper that we had watched climb the wall up the kitchen house of our 'old rat's nest' home.

But the snake which followed the visitors through the front door of our new house was another matter. Three feet long and marked as poisonous by his triangular, pit viper head, he moved into the room on the heels of our visitors. In a flash, the three of them had plastered themselves against the far wall. Now, it had been my pride to trowel that thin cement floor smooth, and that snake would have needed four wheel drive and ABS brakes to make good progress on it. Louise was aghast at its lack of manners.

"I'll kill it," she decided. And then the missionary in her added, "but I will need to be careful with a machete or I am likely to chip my prized new floor." Iyende quickly brought a knife from the kitchen, and Louise stood, foot raised, in the middle of the floor in the pathway of the struggling snake. As the snake's head passed under her foot, she stepped firmly on it. Then cautiously sawing back and forth with the butcher knife, she severed the challenger's head. Nice going, Mrs. Missionary!

The word must have gotten out to the snake community, for this snake was one of only two that sneaked into our new house, the other being the cobra in the living room. And you thought Psalm 91:13 was out of date: "Thou shalt tread upon the lion and the adder: the young lion and the dragon shalt thou trample under feet."

INVADED BY DRIVER ANTS

Bafumba, they are called in the local African language. "Incredible!" you might exclaim when you see the ground so thoroughly covered that the grass seems only a swarming brown mass of ants killing everything in its path. Or you might watch them crossing a trail in the jungle, maybe six or eight columns wide, with their large-headed soldiers sweeping pincers held high as the army marches between them. Hours later when the last of the uncountable host has disappeared into the forest, a deep pathway worn across the trail is evidence that a multitude of feet have passed that way.

On the other hand, you could find them encamped in the jungle: sand, soil, and leaves mulched together forming a canopy over the massed millions gathered there in the darkness. Driver ants are indeed awesome, but also irresistible upon attack. They swarm through trees and across the ground, take over houses in their numbers, and consume whatever is unable to run before them—including, on rare occasions, wounded or disabled human beings.

One night, they marched on us. Norma, our new coworker, had recently arrived from the United States via Switzerland where she had studied French. What a blessed addition she was to our little Gospel task force, coming to help us in the establishment of our schools and adult literacy classes without which our churches would be filled with illiterate people. She had been with us for just a few weeks when the *bafumba* struck.

Silently they swarmed out of the jungle just behind our house. They spread out under cover of darkness, blanketing the ground. Everything fled in terror before their silent advance marked only by the scurrying of insects, spiders, roosting birds, snakes, mice, and rats. All the denizens of the soil, trees, and grass were suddenly in deadly danger. Desperation mixed with resignation reigned as the army moved aggressively forward, overwhelming their victims and dissecting their prey. No sound, did I say? Perhaps the sharpest of ears could discern an almost ethereal hiss, the movement of uncountable tiny feet in concert on a mission to fumigate an entire area.

So it was in the obscurity of an African night where there are no street lamps, no glow on the clouds of nearby towns, no ambient light of floating photons—nothing but deep darkness and the sounds of night birds and insects—that the *bafumba* advanced.

They quietly surrounded our house and probed for an entrance. They moved up the outside walls, blanketing every square inch and pouring into the ceiling crawl space. Advance scouts found a small opening in the back wall at foundation level—just a small spot left unplugged in the bathroom wall where we expected to eventually put a toilet. A horde followed, and soon the bathroom wall had turned into a moving mass. They poured out into the hallway, and then for some reason turned left into Norma's bedroom instead of right into ours.

Unheard, they painted themselves over the walls, the ceiling, the floor—and then, her mosquito net. They found their way inside and into the bed. She stirred in her sleep.

"What in the world is going on? What a horrible dream!" In the next instant, reality struck—there in the dark, with no light switch to flip—this was no nightmare. "Biting somethings" had covered her bed! I will not try to describe the sound that brought us to her rescue; you must imagine it for yourself.

Grabbing my flashlight, we rushed to her door, popped it open, and stared at the amazing sight of a 'moving' room. *Action!* Get the ant spray. Find the entrance. Ah, the hole in the bathroom wall. *Take that, you unwelcome invaders!* Retreat, eh? That's it, retreat!

Their entrance blocked, we turned our attention back to the room, killing a bucketful of *bafumba*. Fortunately, they are not poisonous, just painful—though deadly if you have no way to escape. Next we moved outside, where we used one of the most effective weapons available: sour-smelling cassava flour which destroys their ability to follow their leader's scent trail and breaks up the cohesiveness of the army. Sprinkling cassava flour all around the house drove them back.

And so it was that an hour later we had turned back their attack. But to our dismay, we discovered that the *bafumba* had also entered our kitchen house. There they had found the little bustard (prairie chicken) we were raising, its leg tied with a string to keep it from wandering away in the night. All that remained now was a pile of beak, feathers, and claws. The *bafumba* had also effectively rid us of cockroaches and other unwanted little creatures in the ceiling crawl space. Norma, however, was little worse for the wear of having been so dramatically introduced to the African *bafumba*.

Incredible are some of God's creatures. We got to know them while living as 'jungle rat' missionaries in our thatched roof mud and stick house, but God provided wonderful protection day after day. "Thou shalt not be afraid for the terror by night," says our God in Psalm 91:5 coupled with verse 10: "There shall no evil befall thee." His angels did indeed "keep us in all our ways." (Verse 11)

IYOLOMBO

Neither the Belgian Government nor the missionaries had enough personnel to establish schools in all of the hundreds of villages hidden in the interior of the heart of Congo. Those children intent on getting at least a modicum of education were forced to seek a boarding school. Some of these boys came from miles away to our school at Nkole Nkema. From the Bankutu people no girls came, basically because their parents saw no need for a girl to learn to read. She was going to spend her life planting and harvesting cassava or rice gardens, damming streams to catch fish, and making as many babies as possible.

Iyolombo spent arduous days trekking on foot from Bosandja to Nkole Nkema. Initially, he was bent solely on getting an education, but soon he met the Lord Jesus as His God and Savior, and became serious about serving Him. He advanced to the sixth grade and was an outstanding student. Back and forth over that seemingly endless, danger-haunted trail he went from Nkole Nkema to his village for vacations and returned to school again. Especially important was his presence at Bosandja during the dry season when the new gardens were cut. His people practiced slash and burn agriculture as they had for centuries and as they continue to do today. Because of the poor quality of the soil in these jungle areas and the total unavailability of fertilizer, each family is forced to clear a new patch of jungle each year in order to get a good crop. Why? you may ask. The problem is that once the tropical soil is exposed to Congo's torrential rains, many of the nutrients are washed away or driven deep down. The blazing sun adds to the problem by baking the nitrogen out of the soil. In practical terms this means the soil is exhausted after one crop and useless for a second season.

Consequently, each family fells a new plot each year for a couple consecutive years. By the third year the first plot is covered with new tree and shrub growth perhaps ten to twenty feet high. It can then be felled again, left to dry, burned and replanted to get another crop, albeit not usually as good as the original. Clearing the land is a man's job. Planting and harvesting is a woman's. Iyolombo was needed during that time of the year, so he came and went until it seemed his feet could find their way undirected up and down the hills, through the swamps, and across the rushing streams on swaying stick bridges. He saw the many jungle birds and beasts during these days and came to know the folks in the villages along the way. Some of them were his extended family: aunts, uncles, and cousins. They would usually have something to say about his life, for he was not free to do as he pleased, not having the decision-making independence to which we are accustomed.

Nothing seemed unusual when Iyolombo left on this particular Christmas vacation. We expected him back by the middle of January just as he had always faithfully appeared. But this time was different. Come the beginning of the new school year, there was no Iyolombo in sight. Watching the trail daily, we tired of the waiting and with heavy hearts concluded that Iyolombo, the seemingly faithful, indefatigable young man had fallen by the wayside. Three months passed and there was no sight of Iyolombo. Our eyes no longer searched the road up from our station through the grove of trees where our little clinic was built. Beyond it the dirt road ran up an incline through the grasslands and disappeared into miles of deep jungle.

But one day, reappearing out of that dark jungle and marching purposefully into our Christian village, Iyolombo came back—foot weary and happy to be once again at his spiritual birthplace.

"What in the world happened?" was the question on all of our tongues. His answer was an incredible story of love.

You see, when he arrived at his home village of Bosandja his father was nowhere to be seen. "*Tata na ngai ajali wapi*? (Where's my dad?)" he queried. Then he learned his father had been taken to prison for having killed an elephant without a license. He had succumbed to one of the great temptations and challenges of manhood. If you killed an elephant, you become eligible to wear the copper wire necklace with a specially carved oil palm seed—the proud symbol of a real man. I was given such a necklace by admiring tribal men when my elephant, a dangerous rogue, went down and the entire village feasted[1]. Now Iyolombo's father had slain his elephant and was going to pay with a prison sentence for not having a license. Licenses were a nuisance, extremely expensive, and difficult to secure. Besides, "Who gave the right to these white men to come into our jungle and bind us with this foolishness?"

Perhaps his father had slain the elephant with a spear while smeared from head to foot with elephant droppings to hide the human smell. He would have slipped up in tiny incremental steps with many

---

1 "Rogue Elephant", pg. 57

pauses of deathly stillness until at last he stood behind the elephant, stepped between his hind legs, and thrust the spear with all his might into the soft underbelly of the beast that towered over him. With a cry of agony and rage the elephant might have swung upon him to run him down, but the spear would have torn great swaths through his heart and the elephant would have begun at last to stagger and then collapse.

It could be that his father had used another method, perhaps more cunning but not so brave. The elephants have regular highways through the jungle by which they traverse their most-liked paths and enter their favorite feeding areas. These paths sometimes lead to their death. Iyolombo's father could have taken a short, heavy piece of log, inserted a length of a large headed, well-sharpened spear, and raised that lethal dart high above an elephant trail. Stringing a rope woven with the *nkosa* vine fiber from where a trip lever held the spear to a similar trip line across the trail, a trap was set for the elephant. Unsuspecting, placing his right hind foot into the print of his left forefoot, rhythmically moving down his well-worn path, the elephant would trigger the trip line and the spear would plunge with great force, striking the elephant between the shoulders and dropping him in his tracks.

Or Iyolombo's father might have used a muzzle loader with a heavy charge of black powder tamped down by a wad and loaded with a spear. The spear shaft would have been cut to the right length and shaved until it passed nicely down the barrel. The point of the spear-head would have been cut off to form a chisel shape and then honed razor sharp. That spear, though so difficult to aim it required a closeup shot, would drop an elephant. Sometimes such spears were never found again after firing, having traveled clear through the elephant to dart here and there through the jungle and finally bury themselves.

However he killed his elephant, he was now going to pay for it in prison. Iyolombo was worried about the prison—not that his father had not merited punishment, but that he might not survive it. Prison in Congo was not just a cell and poor food. Prison was brutally hard labor, such as carrying half barrels of water up the steep grade from the stream to the jail between two men all day long. Beyond that, prison was the whip. Twelve or so feet long, it was made of heavy hippopotamus hide tanned to a snakelike pliability. Uncoiling through the air like an angry serpent it whistled with terrible power upon the bare backs of the prisoners lying on their faces. Three strokes every morning was the standard. Three strokes was as much as a man could take.

His father could not survive that backbreaking labor and the awful whip. He would die in prison. "I must see the white official," Iyolombo reasoned. "I must present my offer to him."

The Belgian prison official was astounded, but full of admiration as Iyolombo outlined his plea.

"My father is guilty of breaking the law, but he is too old to survive the hard labor and the whip. I do not come to plead for forgiveness; the crime must be punished. What I come to ask is that I be allowed to take my father's punishment for him. Let my father return to his village. Put me in his cell, give me his hard labor, and let me bear his three lashes every morning. Let me serve out my father's three-month sentence."

Agreement was reached. His father was released, and Iyolombo served his prison sentence. The marks of the whip were upon his back, but he was once again with us at Nkole Nkema and his beloved school. What a beautiful picture of redemption! The story of Iyolombo was used again and again across the area in evangelistic services as an illustration of the love our Lord Jesus demonstrated as our Redeemer.

"Redeemed, how I love to proclaim it; Redeemed by the blood of the Lamb!"

"Giving thanks unto the Father, which hath made us meet to be partakers of the inheritance of the saints in light: Who hath delivered us from the power of darkness, and hath translated us into the kingdom of His dear Son: In whom we have redemption through his blood, even the forgiveness of sins." (Colossians 1:12–14)

"And walk in love, as Christ also hath loved us, and hath given himself for us an offering and a sacrifice to God for a sweetsmelling savour." (Ephesians 5:2)

"Herein is love, not that we loved God, but that he loved us, and sent his Son to be the propitiation for our sins." (I John 4:10)

NO MONEY, NO WORK, NO SCHOOL

Our family lived on $28 a month that first term in the Belgian Congo. Our total monthly support averaged $168 the first six years we spent there. Of our support, $140 went into the work. To put most of your money into your work was common practice for our generation of missionaries, so our decision was not unusual. For us, God's work was our work—our life.

The $28 we kept for ourselves bought flour, sugar, powdered milk, palm oil, rock salt, rice, occasional field corn or sweet potatoes, and always the cassava root. We baked a loaf of bread once a week on Saturday and ate it on Sunday, our American-style meal for the week. The palm oil, so saturated that it is solid at room temperature and must be heated to pour, took the place of butter, margarine, and cooking oil. Louise boiled the rock salt to remove the impurities and turned it into table salt. I hunted our meat, everything from pigeons to elephant. We ate the leaf of the cassava plant seven days a week as our basic vegetable for six years. Using flour sacks, Louise sewed two new shirts for me each year, one for Christmas and one for my birthday. I liked ones with flower prints best. My mother's packages sent from the USA were a Godsend for our children's clothing. We lost considerable weight once we left the States.

For our second term we came back to Congo with more financial support, but the work had grown and our financial situation was still strained. By this time, thirteen churches in various stages of development and seven schools were scattered across our area. Our Bible Institute flourished until there were a total of thirty-six men involved; some were pastors, others were evangelists and trainees. The expenses of this widespread ministry were seemingly beyond our resources.

A serious problem arose when our primary school teachers, under the leadership of our headmaster, Mwanza Moise, complained about needing more pay. That they were indeed paid low wages was not to be denied. On the other hand, we were living about as close to the edge financially as we could survive. It was evident we did not have the funds to raise the teachers' pay, and I demonstrated that fact with diagrams and figures on the blackboard in one of the school rooms. "Balderdash!" was the consensus of opinion. The white man is always rich and can certainly afford higher pay for his teachers. After gaining independence[1], beatings of white men and sexual violence against white women and girls by a mutinous army had also tainted the Congolese view of whites. Independence intimated to them that certain formerly acceptable jobs were now beneath them, and the evidence of their struggle to define themselves was plain to see. Their world had been turned upside down, independence was a disappointment, and whose fault was it?

Our schools had a recreational period each morning, but the children did not go outside to play. Instead, they had organized marching

---

1   "Independence, Congo Style" pg. 209

and singing. It was during this period for the next several days that they practiced a very special marching song under the direction of their headmaster. On the chosen day they marched up the dirt road from the school complex, stepping smartly and singing as they entered our U-shaped driveway. Swinging around in front of our house, they sang a song (the headmaster keeping the beat) called "No Money, No Work, No School." A strike had been called at a school located a thousand miles from the ocean, deep in the Congo jungles.

To say that Pastor Bekanga was upset is putting it mildly. Bless his heart, he never got over a heart full of love for his missionaries and gratitude to his God for his miraculous salvation. He would have served his church had they not paid him a penny.

"Let us call them together and explain again," I advised. That we did, but to no avail. The teachers adamantly let us know they felt we were hiding income somewhere and were unwilling to pay them more. I have to admit it was a bit discouraging. The wear and tear of the work and the tropics was showing on both Louise and myself. We were physically tired and financially strapped and really did not need a strike on our hands.

"Let's try once more," I suggested to Bekanga, and he agreed. Back to the schoolhouse we went. The result was the same.

"Your *Mputu* (their name for the white man's country) is a rich country and they would not send you with such a small pittance of money." "No Money, No Work, No School" remained the theme. It was evident we were at a serious impasse.

"In that case," I said, "let me propose a solution. Let us put this question to God. Bekanga and I will go to prayer and we will ask God to judge between us in a way that will show very clearly who is in the right."

For the next week we waited upon God for His decision. It came early one morning in those darkest moments before the dawn. Our bedroom window faced the Christian village a hundred or so yards down the road. I awoke to red light dancing in the bedroom. I ducked out from under our mosquito net and stepped to the window. Flames were leaping to the sky; someone's house was on fire. I flew into my clothes and raced out the door. Hurrying to the village I could hear the cries of alarm and screams of terror. Dashing towards the flames, I could see that they came from the cooking house of Mwanza Moise, the headmaster—the house in which his children slept.

Mwanshimba, his wife, was rolling on the ground weeping for her children. Cries could be heard from inside the house, its grass roof blazing. The children were trapped away from the only door and were going to die unless the God of Heaven intervened. Tall, gangly Mwanza was struggling with the men who were trying to prevent him from entering the fire-engulfed house.

"Bring axes!" I cried. Two quickly appeared. "Give me one and you take the other," I designated. "Now cut down the inside of the end pole of the front wall, and I will cut the other. Do it quickly!"

Now, you understand that mud and stick walls are built using sharpened poles driven into the ground. Heavier poles stand at each corner and either side of the doorways. A checkerboard of reeds runs parallel to the ground on both sides of the poles and mud is pressed between them, filling the walls. Cutting those vine-tied reeds from top to bottom at the corner poles causes the entire wall to topple, which we did, using the ax handles as a fulcrum at each corner. The children tumbled out, air rushed in, and the entire house went *whoooosh!*

Need I add the obvious? The strike was effectively over. A day or two later we gathered with Mwanza Moise and the teachers, whose thinking was now crystal clear. We met with the Christian village leaders, Pastor Bekanga, deacon-evangelists Ilonga, Ituku, Iyende, and Ndjoko, who heartily agreed to help Mwanza build a new house. The preparation of the necessary materials was arranged with various of the Christian men, some getting poles, some getting reeds, others obtaining the *nkodi* vine, and still others the raffia palm leaves with which a new roof would be plaited. The supply of needed materials grew daily.

While the men erected the frame of the house using the *nkodi* vine, split in four sections with the centers stripped out to leave the tough, pliable fiber for tying, other men plaited the roofing thatch. Meanwhile the Christian women dug a pit where they could mix the thick mud with which the walls would be filled. Thus in record time a new house stood ready for dedication, and a subdued, wiser headmaster gave thanks to the God Whom he now knew better for His justice and His mercy.

And a young missionary couple, tested but rewarded for their trust, knelt in gratefulness to their omnipotent, sovereign, holy, and loving God for the demonstration of His watchful care. Psalm 91, known as The Missionary Psalm, has some reassuring promises: "I will be with him in trouble," "No evil shall befall thee," and angels are charged to "keep us in all our ways."

INDEPENDENCE: CONGO STYLE

Never before had we seen so many trucks passing our mission outpost at Nkole Nkema on the one lane dirt road which ran by us going from east to west. Independence was in the air, and the trucks were filled with personnel from numerous political parties bent on cajoling the jungle people into joining their party. Incredulous, we watched and listened.

According to some of these people, independence was a man of great riches. After the magic day of June 30, 1960[1], this man would come with caravans of trucks loaded with all the good things of this life; everything the white man ever had and much more. Our schools emptied of children; their parents were convinced independence would bring an injection or pill which would enable every child to learn all there was to know in three days. The paths from the villages to the graveyards were cleaned and broadened, the better to insure that the dead upon rising would easily find their way back to their villages.

The people were told that only those holding membership cards

---

1 See "Bima! Bima! Irene Ferrel", pg. 267, for a detailed account of Congo's history and independence from Belgium.

in the political parties could participate in this glorious event. Unfortunately the cards were rather expensive, equivalent to an entire month's pay for many of the men, or to the sale of much fish and meat. In the midst of this bizarre scene we—their missionaries—watched and wondered. Our remonstrations with the people that these men were deceivers coming only to rob them in their innocence were met with comments such as, "What does a white man know about independence? Did a white country ever get independence?" Thus put effectively on the sidelines, we continued to watch and wonder.

Then *he* arrived in our nearest village, Nkole Nkema. *He* was one of two young men who had passed a few weeks ago in quest of a job at the palm oil plantation run by Unilever Company at Bongemba, a village about one hundred fifty miles up the road to the northeast. Big dump trucks made their way up there on occasion, sinking in the great mud holes and skidding on slippery red clay roads dozed up and down the jungle hills. Word was out that drivers were needed. One of the two young men got a job, and the other fellow was on his way back out of our territory.

At Nkole Nkema a brilliant idea crossed his mind, then came back and settled. These people, already duped by the political parties, were set up for a scheme that would make life enjoyable for him. Yes indeed, very enjoyable.

"I am the representative of President Joseph Kasavubu, the father-to-be of our independent Congo," he declared to the credulous villagers. "He has sent me to lead you in the construction of an air strip which will make it possible for him to come personally to meet you people face to face. We can put Nkole Nkema on the map!"

In the villagers' befuddled state this scheme seemed to be the most wonderful thing that had ever happened to their village. Think of it—a personal representative, a *planton* of Kasavubu! They immediately presented him with their guest house, previously reserved for Belgian officials and other white travelers. They sent men to hunt for him, women to bring wood and water, young ladies to supply his every wish, and whomever he wished to serve as his lieutenants. A king could not have been treated with more willingness and eager service.

He went to work immediately delegating authority, sending out messengers to nearby villages to recruit laborers, and surveying the land for an airstrip. Never had the village worked so hard. No Belgian official had ever put them through such strenuous labor. Men, women, children, youth, and older people armed with shovels, hoes, machetes, and axes cleared a great swath of *bongondo* trees, leveled clay termite mounds, and filled tree stump holes. A landing strip magically began to appear out of what had been rough, uneven grassland with seven-foot termite towers and tangled trees. This young man was in heaven. His servants snapped to attention at his every wish; the young ladies were entirely pliant; the whole village was at his command.

Now, he had told them if he ever left, he would go magically and they would not see him leave. Nor did they. For one day a truck pulled in from Bongemba, and guess who was driving? That's right, the other young man. Before the arriving friend could reveal the truth, "Kasavubu's representative", architect of the wonderful landing strip, had snatched a bicycle and was seen pedaling as if his life depended on it toward the Kasai River thirty kilometers away. Minutes later, proving that the fellow's life did indeed depend upon his fleetness and endurance, a group of very angry men armed with spears and machetes thundered past our outpost on foot and bicycles.

They told us upon returning that they had almost caught him.

211

When they arrived at the river bank, having raced after him on the sandy road through the plains, the forest, and the cassava gardens before descending the rough jungle road to the Kasai, they saw him well out into the river in a dugout canoe paddling to safety on the other side.

You would have thought the incident might have awakened them from their independence stupor. But no. The day before independence, June 29, 1960, every door in the village but one was tied with vines on the inside, and with other vines binding it on the outside. The bravest man in the village was the one left to finish tying the last door on the outside. He slept dangerously, with his door tied only on the inside, there being no one left to fasten the outside of his door. That night every citizen of Nkole Nkema, and very likely every other village in the area, lay down fully clothed on their hard, palm branch bed, with political party membership cards under their heads. Doubtless many did not sleep at all for the uncertainty of the situation.

Independence Day dawned as had every other day in the year 1960, and nothing was different. The bravest man in the village cautiously crept from his hut. The village street was broad and sandy, just like yesterday. Lizard tails dragged behind their owners had made the usual skittered markings. The scrawny chickens still clucked and crowed and pecked at the bugs. Dog droppings were still here and there. Doodle bugs (called ant lions by some) still waited at the bottom of their inverted sand cones for the unwary insect to fall to the bottom and be captured by their sharp jaws. The witch doctor's altars were still at the sacred spots, marked by plantain trees leaning heavily with great bunches of cooking bananas. The poles were still there that had carried in the leopard killed last week. The leopard was tied so that he appeared to be walking, as was customary for revered animals. Stacks

212

of firewood carried in from the cassava gardens still leaned against the huts, and the little cooking fires still smoldered. No resurrected dead were in evidence. "I wonder if perhaps they could not find the way," he thought. But no, nothing was different. The village looked this morning as it had yesterday morning and the day, the week, the year, the decade, and the century before. Nothing had happened.

Fearful voices called out from inside houses from which they could not leave without his help.

"How is it out there?"

"Just like yesterday," came his weary answer. "Just like yesterday."

So they came forth, household by household, into the reality of independence—a reality they would regret for decades to come. Within two years they would be asking us, "When will this independence business be over and the Belgians come back so things can be as they used to be?"

"Never," was our reply. But you haven't seen anything yet.

Independence, Congo style—this was just the beginning of a sad, sad tale for the country now called Democratic Republic of Congo. Real problems bubbled and boiled over in the next four years as civil war broke out with a communist invasion that intended to overthrow the newly installed independent government. We sought to steady them through this as we lived with them and claimed Psalm 46:1, 7. "God is our refuge and strength, a very present help in trouble...The Lord of hosts is with us; the God of Jacob is our refuge. Selah."

IF JUDGMENT BEGIN AT THE HOUSE OF GOD

The village of Bena Bendi is located on the northern bank of the Kasai River below where the Sankuru River flows in from the northeast. About a hundred miles up the Sankuru, to the left as you face the river at Bena Bendi, is our jungle station of Longa.

Bena Bendi is a large village composed mainly of the Baluba tribe. The church there was a big one by village standards and contributed boys and girls to our boarding school located at Nkole Nkema, thirty kilometers interior to the north. It was our experiences with those children which eventually opened the can of worms surrounding the events described in this story.

If you have not been previously aware of the sexual permissiveness, or perhaps better described as the loose sexual morals of many African tribes, it will come as a surprise to you that this is not permissiveness but a way of life integral to the whole picture of finding a mate and all that follows. Wide experimentation, mating dances, parental matchmaking, and so forth are the norm. Jomo Kenyatta was the leader of the Mau Mau terrorists whose violent campaign in Kenya against whites and blacks who associated with whites forced the British government to grant independence to Kenya. Kenyatta became the first president of Kenya, and turned out to be perhaps the most outstanding leader Africa has produced to date. I have often remarked that it would have been greatly to Africa's benefit if Jomo Kenyatta could have been cloned. His book *Facing Mount Kenya,* written about the Kikuyu people of his land, spells out the manner in which his tribe prepared its young people for marriage through an elaborate system including female circumcision and features which would shock the average American—especially the average American Christian. Biblical preaching and teaching opposes and confronts many of those morals, and sometimes God steps in and brings judgment as a result.

Our boarding school dormitories for the boys and girls were separate and spaced a good distance apart. In fact, the girls' dormitory was fenced to keep the boys out. To our dismay, we sometimes found tunnels under the fence, coming from the inside out. So we were not overly surprised when we caught one of the young ladies with her boyfriend. However, we were surprised at her reaction, for she was evidently experienced at selling herself to men on the barges that tied up overnight at the Kasai riverbank (a short, steep walk from Bena Bendi). Expulsion was a given, and soon afterwards, we closed the girls' section of the boarding school.[1] The larger questions were "What was going on at Bena Bendi? Who was using these children?"

Alas, over the next several years all of our efforts to elicit information from the church members were in vain. This was despite several disciplinary actions administered, such as strictures concerning

---

1   Louise provides some explanation for why the school was closed: "As long as the girls were there, we would experience problems. The girls would be open to 'suitors', and they would be 'entertained'. We had no problem with our boys' boarding school; the girls, however, were not from our tribe, so we were not as involved with them as we would have been with our own tribal girls."

baptism and the Lord's Table. The only outcome was that we discovered another facet of the illicit activities going on. Evidently, some of the old women in the church were making corn beer. The procedure required the women to thoroughly chew dried corn, masticating it to a fine pulp. They would spit this mash into a large pot and add water, certain aromatic spices, and wood chips. Fermentation turned this mixture into a potent beer which sold well on the barges that paused at Bena Bendi on their week-long journeys to and from southeastern Congo. These huge barges were the transportation backbone of the nation, and the great paddle wheel steamers often pushed three to five of them loaded with hundreds of people and every imaginable type of cargo. To describe them as a zoo would be no exaggeration.

Unfortunately, no one in the church was willing to implicate anyone, especially the person who was responsible for bringing such sin into the congregation. The only solution was to catch someone in the village red-handed. So, very early one Sunday morning, I left Nkole Nkema by bicycle for the thirty-kilometer trek to Bena Bendi. It would have been much easier to go by Jeep, but any guilty party would have heard me coming and have had ample time to hide the evidence. Naturally, it being Sunday, I did not carry the .22 rifle which was usually found slung over my shoulder. And naturally, the antelope sensed that on Sunday the missionary was no threat to their peace of mind, so they stood idly by and watched me as I passed.

I reasoned that there was a little time for some fun when I noticed a doe feeding fifty to a hundred yards off the road. She had not taken note of my approach, so I laid my bicycle down and slipped into the grass. Moving only when she had her head down, I came closer and closer until at last just a few yards separated us. Her head went down again, browsing on the succulent new grass of the recently burned

217

plain. Very slowly, I stood up. Moments later she raised her head. Staring at me, she pondered the appearance of this object so close. "Was that there a few minutes ago?" she asked herself, her white tail twitching as she stared. *"Boo!"* I exclaimed, with a quick stomp in her direction. Her first leap was straight up, her second covered many feet, and within seconds she had accelerated to top speed, bounding this way and that through the grass. "I wonder how she will explain her haste to those she passes," I chuckled.

Back on my bike, I continued onward over the rough, sandy, winding road until at last I descended into the jungle that would carry me to the water's edge. Around the first descending bend I went, struggling now with the deep sand that bogged down many a truck carrying its load of oil-bearing palm nuts. I passed the cassava fields cut from the forest and the little clusters of *bitende,* small acidic pineapples replanting themselves by shoots from the mother plants, growing progressively smaller and sharper in taste. At last I entered the outskirts of the village. Swinging silently down one of the wide, sandy streets I spotted an old woman busily munching on dry corn, the big pot for beer beside her. "I saw you, mother," I declared as my bicycle rolled past. Startled, another old woman lifted her head in time to see me and hear my comment. Sweeping through the village, I spotted several others engaged in the nefarious practice of making corn beer.

Going to the church building and lifting the drumsticks from their place, I began to call the people to church, beating a certain rhythm, "Tut ta-tut ta tut-tut, *yaka na lusambo* (come to church)."

"Come to church!" the drum echoed through the early morning stillness of the village. The people began to gather until at last the church was full. Surprised to see me, wondering why I was there, they nevertheless began the song service and had a good time singing.

218

I rose to speak, turning to the passage in I Peter 4:17, 18 and the phrase "For the time is come that judgment must begin at the house of God..." Giving the Biblical and historical background for the statement and applying it to the present situation, I dealt with the matter of sin in the church. I made clear, direct attempts to help them deal with those who were engaged in the sin, and in particular with whoever was leading the women and girls into evil practices. I expressed my disappointment that they had shown an unwillingness to bring the matter into the open and concluded it must be brought before the God of Heaven for judgment.

My plan, I explained, was to get together with Bekanga Paul, the pastor at Nkole Nkema, and pray with him for God's judgment upon those guilty of spearheading this sin in the church. We would leave it in the hands of God as to what He would do, but we would call upon Him especially to judge the responsible person hiding in the background. After a song and prayer together, I left the village for the return trip to Nkole Nkema.

Through the following week Bekanga and I cried out to the God of Heaven for His cleansing power to fall upon the church at Bena Bendi, and in particular upon the hidden leader. It was Sunday afternoon a week later when the messenger came, peddling hard. Panting and pouring sweat, he pulled up before us.

"*O missionaire, missionaire, yaka noki, yaka noki* (Oh missionary, missionary, come quickly, come quickly)! *Esalemi naino; esalemi naino* (It has happened; it has happened)!"

"What happened?" I asked.

"The person who was spoiling our church (he was a man of twenty-eight) fell dead in the doorway of the church this morning."

"God has spoken," I replied. "We will return immediately."

A church covenant had been prepared spelling out how we as Christians would live for Christ and the sins we would shun as a church. Driving the Jeep now since there was no reason for quiet, I returned to Bena Bendi. The drums spoke again and the people gathered. After speaking to them on purity and faithfulness to the God of Heaven, I presented to them the church covenant. "I want the signature or thumb print of every Christian here who will truly live for the God of Heaven and will turn their backs upon the sin that has so troubled us and caused the death of the leader. Those who will not sign or place their thumb print on this covenant, *get out!*"

With that, about twelve people rose and left the building. With joy and great relief, the others moved forward to happily sign the covenant. The church was cleansed, God began once again to bless, and that church exists today, having gone through the holocaust of the Simba war.

"For the time is come that judgment must begin at the house of God: and if it first begin at us, what shall the end be of them that obey not the gospel of God? And if the righteous scarcely be saved, where shall the ungodly and the sinner appear?" (I Peter 4:17–18)

MONKEY STEW FOR TWO

One hundred and fifty miles of dirt road on a bicycle tends to become a bit tiring. The first couple of miles leaving our 'jungle rat' mission station at Nkole Nkema, we were riding in the plain with a gradual uphill climb. The road was hard-packed fairly well with only occasional stretches of sand. After entering the jungle the trail grew rougher, with roots, fallen trees, water washouts, creek crossings, and so forth. It had been raining quite a bit and some of the hills were muddy. Our vehicle would have had great difficulty surmounting them with so little traction available, and it was hard work to cut enough young trees and branches to gain traction in the deep mud and fill in the gullies which cut across the track. So although we had to supply the horsepower ourselves, it was easier going with a bicycle loaded with saddle bags than it would have been with the Chevy Carryall. On other trips using a Jeep during our second term, we had gone aground on the high center hiding under the muddy water, which left all four wheels spinning. At those moments our five-ton winch came in handy. Locating a stump well ahead, we hooked on and then shifted the winch into action. With the engine idling, the Jeep slid on its skid pan and at last the wheels touched ground and began to roll again.

Baenga had been the first stop Ituku and I had made. There was a good group of Christians in the village, and it was a blessing to have services with them and later sit around a campfire and talk. It was on our way here that we met the 'buzzing snake.'[1] Leaving Baenga, we traveled up and down the jungle hills and did some wading in areas where the heavy rains had swollen the streams to overflowing.

Out of the jungle and into the plains again, Nongimpulu was the next village into which we wheeled our bicycles. Here the villagers hired by the Belgian colonial government as road workers had an easier job maintaining the dirt road. A group of men from each village was responsible for a certain number of kilometers on either side of their village. They filled holes and kept the water runoff ditches clear, tossing the sand and dirt mixture off to the side of the road. This eventually built up a little mound which ran along both sides of the road. In the early morning or evening, Ituku and I would often see partridges and guinea fowl in pairs using the water runoffs as entrances and exits. Especially in the evening, the staccato call of the partridge would often reveal his whereabouts even before we sighted him.

We visited village after village with Gospel services as the miles passed under our wheels. At last we reached our destination, Bongemba. Here the Unilever Corporation had opened two large plantations growing oil palms and cacao. Our church here was large, swollen with workers who had come from other districts. The nearby villages of Dika and Watu also had churches pastored by our national preachers, Bayende and Bolopo. They served faithfully and it was a blessing to share the Word of God with them and their congregations.

---

1 "Itupa, the Buzzing Snake", pg. 73

The only unpleasantness experienced in this area had been finding it necessary to defend an old man who was being beaten by two younger fellows. They decided to leave him alone after I intervened and demonstrated a couple of judo throws on them.

The Belgian director of the Unilever Corporation plantation invited me to stay in his guest house, and then proceeded to make a suggestion.

"I have long wished to sample monkey stew," he said, "but my wife has refused to even allow the meat in the house, threatening to throw out any pot it touches. However," he continued with a twinkle in his eye, "she is now in Europe visiting relatives. If you could secure for me one of the good eating monkeys, my Congolese cook is excellent and could make us what I am sure would be a delicious stew." Enough said!

It took a stroll on the jungle road in an area where the mud caked deep on my shoes, but I finally spotted a troop of *ngeis*. They are one of the more alert monkeys in the forest, but a stealthy approach yielded a nice specimen. When the monkey next appeared, it was in what indeed turned out to be a delicious stew— along with potatoes, no less! Potatoes were too expensive and difficult to secure to be seen on our table. Our first six years on the field was lived on $28 a month, so it was a treat to have potatoes along with the monkey stew.

At the table, the Director had another suggestion to make. "I have an elephant permit," he said, "and I would like you to shoot one for me." News of my .30-06 elephant hunt had evidently reached him.

"I am willing to shoot an elephant for you," I replied, "but only if all of the circumstances are in my favor. On the other hand, I would really rather hunt buffalo, so I will make a deal with you. If I shoot two buffalo and give you one, will you send me, my assistant, our

223

bikes, and my buffalo back to my mission station in one of your trucks tomorrow?"

"It's a deal," was his response.

I added, "If I happen to see an elephant and the situation is in my favor, I'll get that for you too." That night Ituku, Bayende, and I made plans to leave before light the next morning for the hunt. So it was still dark when we stepped onto the path leading from the village of Watu down to the river. The three of us moved with caution in the stillness of the morning.

Wait! Something was stirring on the left side of the trail just ahead. An elephant was feeding in a cassava garden beside the path. Moving slowly, we came abreast of the sound and could just see a dark form moving in the garden. Consulting together, we concluded it was not wise to tackle an elephant in the dark, and so left the jungle giant to his meal.

By the time we reached the river the sun was making its appearance as a glow through the treetops to the east. Wait! There is action up ahead. It turned out to be a group of hippos playing in the water. These monsters of the river were having a time roaring and splashing, though whether in fun or in territorial combat we could not determine. For the moment the river was theirs and we were not about to challenge them for the right of way. Then it grew quiet, and we allowed several minutes as a safety margin before entering the little dugout canoe for the paddle across the river. The splice of jungle between the river and the plains where we might find buffalo having an early breakfast was rather narrow at this point, so we advanced on cat's feet with utmost caution and silence. A heavy fog was just starting to lift as the sun made its presence increasingly known.

We paused just inside the edge of the forest. The tall grass in front of us was lush green, sparkling with dew. The buffalo out there were enjoying prime feed. Standing quietly in a jungle increasingly alive with the sounds of the morning, we waited for the mists to clear a little more before we advanced. There, straight ahead about seventy-five yards away, two dark shapes emerged from the melting fog. The two African Cape buffalo were oblivious to our presence. It seemed the best choice to shoot the one farthest away and hope the thwack of the bullet and jungle echo would cause the second one to run in our direction.

Makalele Monene spoke, and a split second later the bullet dropped the farthest buffalo in its tracks. Just as I had hoped, the nearest one wheeled toward us and headed at top speed for the jungle. Here he comes, filling the scope sight!

Crack!

Makalele Monene barked again and the buffalo wheeled around, legs splaying and elbows out in the beginning of a fall. Then down it came, back to back with the first. In just minutes the hunt was over.

It was a surprised and pleased plantation director who saw us off some hours later in one of his trucks, headed home to Nkole Nkema. Rolling and pitching over the road, the truck gobbled up the miles that had been so laborious on bicycles, and late that afternoon we arrived at Nkole Nkema.

Now came the task of skinning and butchering the huge animal. Out of necessity we had learned that jungle missionary skill, but we had plenty of help too. Soon steaks, roasts, soup meat, liver, and heart were laid out on the drain board of our little kitchen house. A limited amount could be kept in our kerosene refrigerator. The rest would be preserved in our pressure cooker, a task that would keep Louise and her kitchen helper busy for hours at the wood stove. But what satisfaction to see the quart mason jars lined in a row filled with the promise of good eating for weeks to come. Our Christian village would be feasting on the larger portion of the meat that they were given.

"Monkey Stew for Two" had a most beneficial ending. God's greatest gift is His Son, as we read in Romans 8:32, but with Him comes "freely all things." How often we've proved His faithfulness!

THE LITTLE PEOPLE IN THE PHONOGRAPH

It is often heard in church circles that planting churches on the mission field is just like planting churches in the USA. In fact, a more erroneous statement has seldom reached the ears of American Christians. A cursory study of anthropology dispels that notion within a few moments. The fact is that the peoples of the world do not live in different ways in the same world, *they live in different worlds.*

By the way, anthropology was originally a theological concept designed to understand God's most glorious creation, mankind. The idea was stolen from seminaries, for the most part by ungodly evolutionists. Anthropology has been divided into two camps almost from the beginning, the split taking concrete shape with the organization of the Ethnological Society of London. One side believes that all the peoples of the world have a right to the benefits which spin off from healthy human progress. Bible-believing churches and missionaries would be in that philosophical camp. The other side wants to see the various cultures of what might be called the third world preserved unchanged. No Gospel which radically alters their lifestyle and thinking should be foisted on them. That side is adamantly against missions.

When such anthropological individuals (wearing a perpetual frown) show up on our mission fields, at some point in the debate I ask them how they got here. Was it perhaps by raft like the Kon-Tiki expedition, as their ancestors would have crossed the ocean? Was it by prairie schooner, or on foot? Or did they perhaps come by jet? If so, how did they gain the right to be so different from their ancestors? Is their real purpose to keep the jungle peoples in a sort of anthropological zoo so they can be studied by those who benefited by changes they wish to deny the tribal peoples?

"But they have their own religion," they respond predictably.

"They also have their own medical system," I reply. "So why do you champion better health care for them?" Intellectually their mental mousetrap would never capture a single smart mouse, so they don't appreciate our company.

On the other hand, they have learned some valuable lessons and developed insights which can be of immense benefit to the missionary who learns to study his people. Anthropologists have been in the forefront of developing language study methods which have been helpful as well.

How do you deal with Hindus who have no concept of even the existence of sin, and believe there is no reality—that we all live in some kind of dream world? That there is no such thing as a future outside of continuous reincarnation, sometimes for better and other times to enter the animal or insect world? Who believe the most blessed event attainable is passing eventually into nothingness? What do you say to someone who believes that all life is the same life? That plants, insects, birds, reptiles, mammals, human beings, spirits, and thirty million gods all share the same kind of life? Which, combined with reincarnation, forbids them to kill a fly, cow, or rat; even while flies infest their food and rats eat as much as fifty percent of their wheat? These are concepts so unbiblical that they are almost inconceivable to us.

And then there is the caste system, which is really a theological arrangement from the Brahmin who are nearest to god—whoever and whatever that is, for they worship thirty million of them. How about the outcasts who are bought and sold like caged animals?

How do you deal with the African peoples, in whose three thousand languages missionaries and anthropologists have not once found a true future tense, or a word for "everlasting" or "eternal"? They are a people who in all of their history had never produced a prophet or great philosopher, because such a person must have a dream, a utopia, a golden age toward which he is leading his people.

These people believe that immortality is the state of a disembodied spirit (the body in the grave and the spirit floating free) being spoken to by name by someone who had known him while he was in the body. In the Kikuyu language the past is called *zamani*, the present is called *sasa*, and the overlap between these two is a resting place. It is a place of immortality in which a spirit is kept "alive" by having someone who had known him in the flesh come with an oblation (food) or libation (drink) and talk to him, calling him by name. When the last person dies who knew the dead personally and can call him by name, that spirit goes back into *zamani*, back into oblivion—ceasing to exist. How do you talk to a people like that about heaven, eternity, or judgment to come?

No, I think it is evident that we don't live differently in the same world; we live in different worlds. And the job of the missionary is, by the grace of God, to cross into those other worlds and miraculously and laboriously see folks from those worlds transformed into a

229

Biblical people living in a Biblical world. Such an accomplishment is indeed a miracle, and that miracle is missions.

I say all of this to prepare you for what I think is a humorous story, but also one that illustrates that we do, indeed, live in different worlds.

The village of Iyelu is perhaps sixty miles from our station at Nkole Nkema. Bayenga was closer, and we would often stop there overnight on our bicycle trips up that direction. There was (and is) a nice group of Christians in Bayenga, and it was always a joy to spend time with them. Sitting around a campfire in front of the hut in which we slept, we would talk and tell stories and sing long into the night.

Iyelu was a particularly backward village that was extremely resistant to the Gospel. We had come into possession of several hand-wind phonographs with governors on the flywheel. Turning the crank would produce a 78 rpm rotation of the turntable onto which we placed recordings of Gospel songs, preaching, and Bible stories. We placed some of these machines with our national pastors, who used them effectively in spreading the Gospel. It is important for you to understand that the governors on these phonographs were adjustable via a little lever next to the turntable. While turning the crank the operator could adjust the speed so as to get the best sound.

We spent the night at Iyelu after calling the people, those who would come, to a Gospel preaching service. In the morning we were holding another service using the phonograph as an attraction. This was the first time any one of these villagers had ever laid eyes on a phonograph. They were astonished at the voices coming out of it in message and song. "*Lo-ko-to!*" an old man breathed, using his tribe's word for utter amazement. Then an idea struck me. Maybe I could contrast truth with error and prove to them how easily they were deceived by untruth, and break through their resistance to the message of the Gospel. They didn't need to treat it as a deception of the white man intruding upon their ways.

"Do you know what makes that music and who is speaking those words?" I asked the crowd.

"*Te, toyebi te* (No, we know not)," they responded.

"Would you believe that it is little tiny people inside the phonograph?"

"*Soki ejali boye* (Maybe it's that way)," they responded hesitantly.

"Well, let me speak and see if there will be a response," I countered. "Listen."

With that, I again began turning the crank, and the voices spoke. Leaning over the phonograph with my finger on the adjustment lever I spoke to it, my mouth close. "You in there, sing more slowly." With that I pushed the lever toward slow. The voices deepened and slackened their pace. Wonderment buzzed through the crowd. "No, no! Not so slow; talk faster," I instructed the little people and pressed the lever toward fast. Jabbering, the voices hurried on their way through the song.

They were completely convinced. Little people lived in that box and could be spoken to by the missionary. "Do you believe?" I challenged.

"Yes, yes," they shouted.

"Well then," I countered, "you believe a lie because there are no little people in this box. Look, see this lever. Listen to what happens when I push it down, and what happens when I push it up."

"Oh," they said, "so you deceived us."

"Yes, I did, on purpose. You have believed so many lies the devil has fed you through the years, and many of you have died still

231

believing him. We have come as missionaries and told you the truth again and again. Never have we told you a lie. But just now I have proved to you that when we do tell you a lie, you believe it immediately, whereas when we tell you the truth you reject it. Now, let me tell you the truth once again. Listen carefully, for this is the Word of the God of Heaven Who created us and Who would never tell us a lie." With that I once again gave them the Gospel message.

We do indeed live in different worlds. May God enable us to become acculturated into their world and be able by His grace to bring them out of darkness into the glorious light of the Gospel.

"But if our gospel be hid, it is hid to them that are lost: In whom the god of this world hath blinded the minds of them which believe not, lest the light of the glorious gospel of Christ, who is the image of God, should shine unto them. For we preach not ourselves, but Christ Jesus the Lord; and ourselves your servants for Jesus' sake. For God, who commanded the light to shine out of darkness, hath shined in our hearts, to give the light of the knowledge of the glory of God in the face of Jesus Christ." (II Corinthians 4:3–6)

WITCH DOCTOR AT NKEKETE

Louise and I were on a village trek deep in the Isoldu. We set out from Mark Grings' station at Yassa; behind our bicycles followed the men we had hired to carry our two metal trunks.

Two of the villages to which we were going had been built within a couple hours of each other on the same path. We reached Yekeyeke first and made camp there. It was the weekend and we would be there over Sunday. The dirt floor needed to be swept, the goats chased away, and the gates of the "living fence" made up of manioc stalks planted around the government rest house had to be secured. As we worked to complete those tasks, we heard the carriers chanting as they trotted into the village with the cadence peculiar to their profession. The camp cots were untied from the tops of the trunks and set up. Small poles cut from the nearby forest and stuck in the floor at the four corners of the bed provided the means for hanging our mosquito nets. Firewood and water came from the village women; we used these to cook our meals and boil drinking water in the small cookhouse out back.

That evening as the sun was completing its downward journey in the west, we gathered on the broad, sandy street of the village for a service. Some folks came close to hear and others stood afar off, listening as we sang songs of Jesus in their language and preached the Gospel. In the morning we held another service in Yekeyeke, and then biked over to Nkekete. Folks gathered for the service and we let them know we'd be back on the morrow. Sunday closed with the Gospel message preached again at Yekeyeke.

As we approached Nkekete on Monday morning, we were met by women heading out to go fishing. No, you must not imagine it was with a pole, hook, and line. They were going to a forest stream, which they would dam in two places with sticks, leaves, and mud, trapping all of the fish in that area between the two dams. Then some of the women would stand downstream from the lower dam with large baskets, while other women using tighter woven short baskets would bail the water out of the entrapped area. The large baskets held at the dam would act as sieves letting the water through, but holding any fish. Hopefully, they wouldn't also catch one of the poisonous snakes. We let the women know we'd be holding a service, and were glad to see them leave their baskets and follow us back to the village.

A sizable group gathered around us. An old man appeared, evidently a witch doctor, with his son and the son's wife. We began to sing the gospel songs we had translated. No one else listening had any knowledge of them, and ours were the only songbooks in evidence. Few would know how to read. The witch doctor, Boika and his wife, listened particularly intently. It was a simple message dealing with sin and its consequences, the love of God, and the crucifixion of the Lord Jesus Christ—God's Son; how there must be confession, repentance, and faith in the Lord Jesus as Savior and God. These special three were taking it all in. An invitation was given:

"Who listening has realized they are a lost sinner, guilty as

234

charged and worthy of death? Who has understood that *Nzambe*, the God of Heaven who created him, loved him enough to come to this earth, become a man, and die on a cross for his sins? Who would like to receive this *Nkolo Yesu Klisto* (Lord Jesus Christ) as his *Nzambe mpe Mobikisi* (God and Savior)?"

The witch doctor spoke up. "*Ngai mpenja, nalingi* (I myself do)."

Incredulous, I asked him if he had understood, to which he replied in the affirmative.

"*Tika nalakisi yo mbala moko mosusu* (Let me explain that to you again)," I said, and spelled out the picture for him once more. I made it plain that if he turned to the Lord and truly took him as his Savior and Lord, the God of Heaven would take him out of his witch-craft and sin and make a new man out of him. Was he ready for that?

"*Qui monsieur, nalingi* (Yes sir, I want that)."

We took the three adults to the Nkekete rest house. "Kneel with me," I said, which they did. He then confessed his lostness and that he was putting his faith in Christ as his Savior and God. Boika and his wife did likewise. What a joy it was to witness them entering the family of God. Ring the bells of heaven! We were rejoicing, but terror rocked the village. Drums began to beat, people ran to and fro in fear.

"Follow me," waved the newly converted witch doctor as he led us toward his bark-walled, thatch-roofed hut. No bigger than would fit in your bedroom, dear reader, but it was his house. Into it he went and came out with his hands full of the charms and fetishes he had used in a lifetime of service to Satan. Again he disappeared into the darkness of his windowless hut. Arms loaded, he reappeared and added to the growing heap—the trappings of a life lived in bondage and futile effort to appease the *bekadji* (evil spirits) and death. Back inside he went, this time to the little fire which typically smolders

235

in the houses of the Bankutu people. Tendrils of smoke rising from those embers filter through the thatch, preserving and painting it glossy black with carbon.

He brought a hot ember and dropped it into the midst of the tinder dry fetishes. Animal skins, skulls, fangs, and claws of leopard and wild boar, bundles of sacred leaves, gourds filled with unseen items: all these were the tools of his craft, the sum of his close association with his master, Satan. Standing over the heap, this babe in Christ—this former witch doctor—blew upon the hot coal. Smoke began to twirl from the heap, a tentative flame appeared, and then a roaring inferno!

Eyes staring, mouths agape, hearts thudding in fear, the people stood transfixed at a sight they had never dreamed of seeing. Then the new child of God spoke again.

Voice strong with conviction and emotion, he cried, "Do you see that smoke? That is my old life!" You would have thrilled with us that day when the once servant of Satan was so gloriously saved and transformed.

It was an ongoing story. You would have joined in praising God to hear that Boika's brother was also saved. Later Mark made the trip to Nkekete and administered baptism to these "new creatures in Christ." It was the two sons who carried their now feeble father down the jungle hill to the creek in which they were baptized. You would also rejoice to know that Boika and his wife came to live on Mark Grings' station so he could attend Bible School, and to hear Boika Djema preach after he became pastor of his village church in Nkekete. How marvelous it will be to meet them in glory and recall once again the momentous miracle at Nkekete.

236

"Many, O Lord my God, are Thy wonderful works which Thou hast done...more than can be numbered." (Psalm 40:5)

"UNTIL LAST WEEK, I WAS A WITCH DOCTOR"

*Editor's note: This and the following
story take place almost thirty years after
the Champlins had been evacuated, on one
of their return trips to Congo.*

Our journey began with a hundred mile trip down the
Sankuru River from a point located just south of dead center
Africa, the missionary outpost of Longa. Daniel Grings and I set out in
our twelve-foot-long aluminum skiff. Heavily loaded would be a good
but inaccurate description; overloaded would better describe it. Since
no fuel, medicine, or other supplies were available anywhere along
the way, everything we would need had to go in that little boat.

From stem to stern it was packed with boxes of literature, a chop
box with food staples, motorbikes, and tanks of fuel for them and the
boat's outboard engines. A two-man tent, tools for maintenance in
case of engine trouble, a short-wave radio complete with battery and
antenna, spare clothing, and medicines for ailing villagers as well as
ourselves in case of sickness, wounds, or accidents were also included
in the provisions. We would sleep on the ground with a thin blanket
as a mattress and one for cover in the cool of the early morning. A
kerosene lantern and flashlights would provide light. Our raincoats

would come in handy when the skies opened in torrential downpours, but do nothing to protect us from monstrous lightning bolts, whether we were in our little boat or on our motorbikes.

What a sight we made when we tested the boat at Longa with a number of national believers observing from the high river bank. The 30-horsepower outboard engine struggled mightily but was unable to plane the wallowing little boat. It seemed we were pushing more water ahead of us than was passing under us. It was evident that one engine would not do the job. However, by God's provision, Louise and I had been able to bring a 15-horsepower Honda 4-cycle outboard with us on the plane as checked baggage, just as we had brought the 30-horsepower engine on a previous trip. Not cheap, but the only feasible way. Anything sent as freight would most likely have been stolen from the customs warehouse. Since the limit for checked baggage over the ticket counter is one hundred pounds, it was necessary to disassemble the Honda engine. The power head went into a specially built box. The rest of the engine was placed in pieces mixed with other things in two footlockers. We reassembled it after arriving at the jungle station and found it to be in perfect working order.

Now it was time to team it with the 30-horsepower 2-cycle engine and make the little boat go. What a strange sight we were, a squat aluminum boat loaded to the gills with the 30 HP set up to push and steer, and the 15 HP to one side, locked straight ahead to just push. Back into the boat we went. All set? We opened both throttles, and *presto!* the boat planed nicely. Off we went downriver, reading the water as we went, for it was dry season and many a sandbar lurked beneath the surface.

Wending our way from village to village, we dispensed Gospel literature. Many of the sandbars housed little camps of folks spending their time catching and smoking fish. Time and again, dugout canoes filled with eager folks met us mid-river with hands outstretched for the tracts and Bible portions.

At one point, a breeze was blowing which rippled the water and made it much more difficult to determine where the main channel lay. We did not want to run aground and damage the boat or engines—no roadside emergency phones here! Approaching a large sandbar where a number of people were encamped, we found it impossible to determine by the surface of the water on which side the channel might pass. Waving to the men on shore, we indicated by hand signals our question, "Which side do we take?" To the left, they wigwagged. Alas, within moments we drove full speed into water that was but inches deep. Both engines dumped in the ankle deep water and we were indeed aground. Thankfully no harm was done; Dan and I were able to push off, restart the engines, and work our way around the impasse.

On the mission field we laughingly call a place where we can relieve ourselves a Texaco station. Ours that day was a large sandbar with scrub trees and brush toward the center. There we took care of the necessary business and got out our lunch: chicken cooked in delicious orange palm oil along with chunks of a big dumpling made of cassava flour. After a drink of water from our canteens and hands washed with sand and river water, we were on our way again.

At last appeared the familiar red cliffs of high ground near where the Sankuru and the mighty Kasai River come together. Leaving the Sankuru (several hundred yards wide), we entered the mile-wide Kasai and arrived shortly at our riverside destination. There was time still to make our camping site, but a huge bank of dark clouds did not bode well for a pleasant journey. The first part of the trip was uneventful; our bikes purred along the narrow footpath through alternating patches of plain and forest. At one point Dan stopped and pointed with his chin up into the trees. Even in the gloom of the jungle shadows it was a beautiful sight: a whole flock of blue feathered, white speckled guinea fowl scattered like blossoms on the branches of a tree.

Then we were out into the plains again, headed into the approaching storm. Donning our raincoats and hoods proved to be an exercise in futility; nothing would keep the driving rain from soaking our bodies from head to foot. Bolts of brilliant lightning were followed by claps of thunder that rolled across the land. The path became a river and my motorbike stalled again and again as water splashed over the engine. Somehow water was being sucked into the fuel system. A steep hill faced us, where torrents of water were washing out the path as they cascaded downwards. Soon I was pushing my bike, slipping and sliding. Dan laughed—the rascal!—and got out the Super-8 video camera. That is, until his bike bogged down in a miniature canyon and it took the two of us to lift it out. Then the storm was over and the fresh smell of damp earth and grass pervaded the air.

Pulling into the Christian village at Nkole Nkema, we erected our tent, changed our clothes, and hung the wet ones out to dry. A vine stretched between two poles served as our drier. Joyfully, the Christians crowded around with repeated handshakes and many an *mbote* (hello). The next morning saw the church crowded for messages from Dan and myself. Special music had been prepared by the church leadership and school teachers, with African instruments adding melody and rhythm to the singing. We spent hours dealing with problems and counseling with the leadership. Graceful Christian ladies brought water for us from a little jungle stream more than a mile away. Pots black with the soot of open wood fires contained cassava greens as a

242

vegetable and boiled sweet cassava as our starch. Tiny legs and firm, roasted chicken breasts made a tasty but tough entrée.

The next day found us on our way again, stopping to talk with our school teachers in several villages. They are vital men, for without our schools the children of these villages would remain untaught and the next generation of people in our churches would remain illiterate. We found later that some of these teachers had been without pay for several years, and were still teaching while gardening and hunting to supply food and clothing for their families.

It was evening as we approached our next overnight stop. We found Christians putting up new church buildings in two villages, and had services with both groups. After the second service Dan stayed with the people while I went on to set up our tent and make camp for the night. It was dark now, dark as only a remote jungle location can be. In the African jungle there is no ambient light reflecting off the clouds from a nearby town, no street lights, no electricity, no bulbs shining from a window. Because of their poverty the people can no longer afford even kerosene lamps or lanterns. On a special occasion someone might light a torch of pitch, but would not dare take it into his seven-foot-high hut roofed with tinder dry grass or thatch. Thus, the only lights in a village are the little wood fires outside their huts for cooking or perhaps keeping warm on a cool night, and the smoldering fires that burn all day and night inside their huts.

Such a village appeared on my right as I wended my way down the winding path on my bike, lit by its head lamp run by a little dynamo spinning against the front tire. People were gathered around a fire, so I swung off the dirt path into the village and approached them. As soon as my bike stopped, the head lamp went out and we stood talking by the light of the flickering flames.

243

At that moment a short old man stepped out of the darkness. "I was a witch doctor until last week when one of your preachers led me to Christ," he announced in Lingala. What a thrill to hear! But his next statement was even more wonderful. "My wife wants to be saved too; will you talk with her?

"Have her come at sunup tomorrow morning so that we can have time to talk."

She appeared at the rising of the sun. Clouds of light fog still hung over the jungle out of which the village had been cut. "Come sit here where we can talk," I said, and we sat facing each other on little African stools. Around seventy, her face and body worn with the cares of a hard life, she listened intently. From her animist background she knew little about the God of Heaven—the God of the Bible. The strange characters printed on a page might appear to be some kind of magic from the white man's country, called *Mputu* by her people. So we began at God, and for an hour or more talked about Who He is and where He exists. We talked about His omnipotent power, His creation of all things including mankind—including her. His holiness, righteousness, and justice; His hatred of sin and how sin came into the universe and the world through the fall of her father and mother, Adam and Eve. We talked of how she was born a sinner who naturally rebelled against the holy God of the universe, and about how God must judge every sin, the wages of which are death. Then we came to the glorious news of God's love, so great a love that He came as the man (*Jesu Klisto*) so that He could die on a wooden cross and shed His blood for our sin—for her sin. We continued to this holy God's offer of salvation by grace through faith in the Lord Jesus to anyone who would come as a lost sinner appalled by their rebellion, recognize their worthiness of eternal death, ask forgiveness, and receive

244

Him as their God and Saviour. Her attention never wavered and her questions showed clarity. This entire conversation was, of course, laced with illustrations and explanations from the reservoir of her own culture.

"Now, would you like to talk to God about your sin?" I asked.

"Oh yes," she answered and bowing her head began to pray.

"Oh God in Heaven, You are so powerful. You created everything on earth and in the sky. You made Adam and Eve, my father and mother. You made me. And, oh God, You are holy, and You hate sin. You are just and You must judge every sin. And, oh God, I am such a terrible sinner..." (Here she detailed her sins including the worship of false gods, witchcraft, serving Satan, lying and stealing, cursing with a filthy mouth—a litany of rebellion against the holy rule of the God of the universe.)

Then with a broken voice she declared, "I am worthy of judgment, oh God. If You cast me into that terrible lake of fire You are right, for I deserve it. But You loved me and Your son Jesus loved me and died for me on a wooden cross. Thank you, Lord Jesus, for shedding Your blood to pay for my sin. Please forgive me. Oh God, please make me Your child. Please write my name in Your Book of Life."

I sat enthralled at the work of the Holy Spirit taking the Word of God and sending a shaft of enlightenment through the darkness of a life of animism and sin. It broke through the barrier of a lifetime of ignorance concerning the things of God and brought a woman to her Creator and Saviour, glowing with worship and faith.

Incredible! Impossible! Miraculous! *But God!* I wonder if my reader has ever heard a new American convert speak and pray with such clarity when they came to Christ?

Minutes later she and her former witch doctor husband stood

side by side glowing as I took a picture of them. "I was a witch doctor and I was saved last week," he had said. "My wife wants to be saved too; will you talk with her?" Now they were on their way to heaven together, trophies of the grace of God.

"But God, who is rich in mercy, for his great love wherewith he loved us, Even when we were dead in sins, hath quickened us together with Christ, (by grace ye are saved;) And hath raised us up together, and made us sit together in heavenly places in Christ Jesus: That in the ages to come he might shew the exceeding riches of his grace in his kindness toward us through Christ Jesus." (Ephesians 2:4–7)

OH LITTLE GIRL, YOU'RE BLIND

The little aluminum skiff hardly looked up to the task. About twelve feet long, it contained two dirt bikes (a large and a small), fuel for two hundred miles of river travel and sixty by bike, literature, a small short-wave radio, some food and first aid medical supplies, a change of clothing, spare parts, and our two-man tent. No gas stations, clinics, or stores would be accessible, for there were none in the area to which we were going. But Dan Grings and I had done this before, and we knew that two outboard engines teamed up on the transom would do the job and we would be enabled to preach the Gospel in a number of villages both on our way to our destination and on our return trip. So off we went, making our way southwestward down the Sankuru River.

The all-Christian village on the northern bank of the Kasai River, just after the confluence of the Sankuru and Kasai, had been very helpful to us on previous trips like this. After greeting the people and chatting with them for a few minutes, we hauled our boat ashore, removed the engines for storage in a hut, and leaned the boat up against it. With bikes loaded we hit the trail, first passing through the forest with the cassava and banana gardens of the villagers,

247

then breaking out into the plains with the scorching sun beating down on us.

The familiar sight of the grove called Topokatopi came into view across the valley, and then the smaller grove and its cliff down which the Grings family used to go for their water. Topokatopi was home to my wife and her family after her mother's death in 1936. They lived in a small house with mud-plastered lattice work walls; their bedroom was the top of the vine ceiling to which they climbed by a pole ladder. They heard the chilling howl of hyenas during the night and the owls hooting to one another, and knew leopards prowled the forest around them.

The old dirt road which led to Nkole Nkema was overgrown now due to a lack of maintenance for many years. A footpath branched off to the left and Dan and I followed it to our Christian village. An excited group of folks greeted us, glad to have us in their village again. The sun resting on the horizon warned us there was little time left before dark in which to pitch our tent under a spreading palm tree next to some banana plants, think about supper, and hold an evening service. It was in the morning that I went looking for our house up the road from this newly built village. Having been destroyed during the terror of the Simba Rebellion, only two pieces of evidence remained of the dwelling that once stood there: a piece of the back kitchen wall and a cement column which supported the roof overhang on the right front of the house. The cement cistern constructed to store rain water for dry season was deprived of its roof and cluttered with pieces of blocks and frogs. A sad sight!

We were called upon to help the pastor and his leadership deal with a very sad matter. The African male nurse at our clinic was accused of misconduct and had to be dismissed. The church

248

leadership agreed it was the only Scriptural course to be taken, but it meant closing the clinic for lack of a nurse. Our people's access to medical care evaporated. The nearest possible help was now twenty miles away on foot or bicycle and across the two-mile-wide Kasai River. Few would ever be able to make that trip, for getting a patient there would only complicate the condition.

Reality came home with a jolt the next morning when a little girl was brought to us. The cloth covering her head and the right side of her face was filthy. Flies and gnats swarmed around her head which she pathetically tried to wave away with a sweep of her hand. "Her eye is sick; please help us," her mother pleaded. I lifted the cloth and gazed upon a gruesome sight. Her right eye was swollen twice its normal size; pus oozed from her eye socket and lids. But the worst element of this sickening sight was the cornea; it was solid white.

"What happened?" I asked the mother.

"Three days ago she washed her face in a jungle stream and a *bekadji* (evil spirit) grabbed it," she replied. That was a normal response in a culture which believes sickness is caused, not by infection, but by an evil spirit's maliciousness.

Taking my Super-8 video Handycam, I recorded several macro color pictures on the film. What can I do for her? I have some of my own tetracycline eye salve that might arrest the inflammation. But my heart was saying, in tears, "Little girl, you are blind in that eye— undoubtedly blinded. I hope whatever was in that stream does not affect your other eye."

"Wash that cloth," was my stern instruction.

"How can they think it helps to cover it with something as filthy as that?" my thoughts stormed.

"And little girl, keep your fingers out of your other eye, lest infection cause the same thing to happen to it! Do you understand?"

Easy, missionary; don't let your frustration get out of hand. Perhaps if you'd been born and raised in such mental and material darkness, such things wouldn't be easy for you to understand either.

Oh, little girl, you're blind in that eye—so young! And the clinic is closed. I hope I find a doctor who by looking at my pictures will be able to determine what caused it and the treatment for it, so next time I'm in these villages I'll know what to do and be prepared to do it.

In the meantime, the clinic is still closed for lack of a nurse. Is it possible someone out there who reads this might hear the Spirit of God say to them, "I want you there"? Oh, little girl, you're blind, while our nurses work in stainless steel hospitals far from the reality of the great need of your people. Will someone come? Oh, little girl you're blind, and I don't know of anyone who might come.

STORY EPILOGUE 1

To the glory of God, a nurse in Harrisburg, Pennsylvania read this challenging plea and responded. She gave up her comfortable position in her "stainless steel hospital" and came to serve in a very simple little clinic with minimal facilities with which to work. Isaiah 30:21 encourages us, "Thine ears shall hear a word behind thee, saying, This is the way, walk ye in it..." Medical ministry has been greatly used of God as a door opener for the preaching of the Gospel.

STORY EPILOGUE 2

Sad to say, I did discuss this case with a specialist in the USA. His diagnosis was that this particular kind of eye infection without immediate, intensive treatment most likely invaded the brain and killed the little girl within days.

Oh, little girl you're blind. Oh, little girl, you're dead.

"But when he saw the multitudes, he was moved with compassion on them, because they fainted, and were scattered abroad, as sheep having no shepherd. Then saith he unto his disciples, The harvest truly is plenteous, but the labourers are few; Pray ye therefore the Lord of the harvest, that he will send forth labourers into his harvest." (Matthew 9:36–38)

TERROR IN CONGO

By 1964, the Nsimbas[1] had been the scourge of Congo for two years. They were a product of the circumstances which resulted in the premature independence of the land of the Belgian Congo. Riots in the larger cities had induced panic in the Belgian government, causing them to give independence to a country of fourteen million that reportedly contained only one university graduate. The horde of young men with a sixth grade education believed independence would be heaven on earth. In fact, many of the jungle people believed independence was a man coming with convoys of trucks loaded with all the good things of life. Children dropped out of school because their parents had heard that independence would bring an injection that would enable the children to learn everything in three days! Such rumors were foisted on the people by the political parties vying for supporting members. The result was immediate chaos, political warfare raging between bitterly opposed tribal-based parties, and the attempted secession of the Katanga Province to the south, put down only with the help of United Nations troops. The Congolese forces in the Belgian-led army

---

1   The Swahili name for "lion", otherwise referred to in this text as "Simbas".

mutinied against their officers and a horror of rape and pillage followed. The country tottered on the brink of anarchy and the economy collapsed. Within a four-year span inflation rocketed 900%. Jobs became non-existent and the bitter, disillusioned, ill-educated youth were ready for revolt.

That revolt came in the form of the Simba Revolution, led by Mulele Pierre and a cadre of young men trained in insurgency by mentors in Communist Eastern Europe. The Simbas intended to destroy the Belgian Congo as they had known it in preparation for a utopia to be brought in by their Communist friends. Congo, the western bulwark in Africa that blocked the advance of Communism toward rich, important South Africa, was in danger of falling into its hands. The Simbas surged across the country, looting, plundering, raping, killing, and burning. Smoke rose from factories, government buildings, police stations, stores, schools, hospitals, and plantations. Bridges were burned, ferry boats were sunk, roads deeply trenched then covered with a thin disguise of sticks and sand. Ambushes became common; people suspected of being Belgian or Portuguese were killed. Then America entered the war on the side of Mobutu, the anti-communist dictator who had ascended to rule over the bodies of his opponents. "Save Congo from Communism!" was the battle cry. Then attacks began against Americans.

By 1964 we had been in the midst of this chaos for two years. Our family was spread over an area more than four hundred miles wide: Mark was at Yassa to our northeast, Louise and I were in the middle, and Louise's older brother Bob and his family occupied a mission field to our west. We had determined to stay with our people.

Traveling became difficult, sometimes requiring detours around burned out bridges, to say nothing of roads badly deteriorated from lack of maintenance. On occasion when traveling at night, we would find a log across the narrow one-lane dirt road. In the dark we knew rebels were watching from high banks around us to see if we warranted death. Had they heard a word of French, Flemish, or Portuguese from our mouths, they would have killed us. Upon hearing us remark in their language through rolled down windows, "Why are these people blocking the missionaries from returning to their station?" they merely watched as we got out of our vehicle, rolled the log out of the way, and passed on into the night.

The terror continued. Never to be forgotten is Davidi, one of our young teachers. He went to his village of Bena Bendi, thirty kilometers from our Nkole Nkema station, to visit with his family for the weekend. Monday arrived and he was nowhere to be seen, his classroom unattended. Friday came and at last Davidi rode in on his bicycle.

"Where in the world have you been?" was my irritated exclamation.

With that he began to weep. "Sir," he said, "when I arrived at my village on Friday evening my mother and brother were missing. We looked for them all day Saturday, with no success. Sunday morning found us out again, searching. At last on Sunday afternoon we found them floating, tied face to face, in the Kasai River. After releasing the bonds, we found their hearts had been cut out."

In January 1964, we were gathered together as an entire family at the Iwungu station[2] with Bob Grings. Mark had been under house arrest in his area for some weeks, and had at last been allowed to leave. Coming to our place by motor bike over the jungle trails, he joined us on our trip over to Iwungu on December 31, 1963, a two-hundred-mile trip that lasted from early morning to late night and included three

2   Iwungu was located between Kikwit and Idiofa. See map on pg. xii.

ferries. Such trips were made twice a year to get together as a family and plan the home schooling of our children. Louise and I needed medical attention as well at this time, so we traveled on from Iwungu to a missionary medical facility about ninety miles away, while our children remained at Iwungu with the rest of the family.

It was then that the Simba Revolution erupted in a volcano of violence across the area. We were cut off from our relatives and our children, David, Jonathan, and Deborah. Rebels stormed into the Iwungu station and placed our entire family under house arrest. Jonathan, nine years old at the time, lived for several years following with flashbacks of the fearful sight of a rebel standing at the bathroom window, his bow drawn. All communication with our family was severed. Rebels controlled the other side of the Kwilu River and beyond. Trees were felled across the roads and the bridges burned. Trapped away from our family, Louise and I joined the rescue effort at the town of Kikwit. UN planes and helicopters arrived to evacuate those in danger.

Using our Jeep truck, I was able to carry fuel to the little airstrip from which the planes operated. Standing on the wings with a bucket and funnel I refueled plane after plane. Louise shared in caring for the refugees as they were brought in and sent to the missionary guest house.

Then one day across the airstrip came one of our missionary brethren. "Brother Champlin!" he cried. "It's terrible, it's terrible! Irene Ferrel has been killed."

Irene and her coworker, Ruth Hege, had been at Iwungu with us just two weeks earlier. Hearing that their beloved national pastor and the Christians at Mangungu were endangered by the rebels, they believed they needed to go back to their people—right into the mouth of the lion. At midnight several days later, the rebels stormed into the mission station screaming "*Bima! Bima!* (Get out! Get out!)" Pushing Irene and Ruth from the house, they shot Irene through the neck and Ruth in the shoulder with arrows. Irene, her blood spouting, exclaimed "I'm finished," and fell to the ground. Ruth, soaked in Irene's blood, lay beside her utterly still. Prodding Ruth and yanking her hair, they tried to determine if she were alive or dead. Finally, leaving her for dead, they looted and retreated. Later, rousing from her God-induced stillness, she crawled into their small garage. There she found a couple bags of dried beans, emptied them, and snuggled down into them, covering herself with the sacks in an attempt to get warm in her state of chilled shock. Christians managed to keep her hidden until she could be rescued by helicopters.[3]

The second time our missionary friend came across the airstrip, he hardly knew what to say. His news was that the UN had reported that our entire family was massacred by the rebels. This included our fellow worker, Norma Jenkins, who had been with us just nine months in Congo.

Our hearts broke, and we heard our Lord speak to us, asking, *"Do you love me? Love me enough to give me your children, your family, for the souls of Africans?"* Our David, raised from infancy in the old mud and stick house. Jonathan, born too suddenly on the bedroom floor of a missionary friend's house twenty miles from the clinic we had expected to reach. Born with the cord around his neck, not breathing. Oh, how we had worked and prayed as we resorted to lowering him into a pan of warm water, then cold, to elicit at least one gasp of breath. At last, he had begun to function. Deborah, darling little Deborah, now six.

---

3   Details of this are to be found in "Bima, Bima, Irene Ferrel", pg. 267.

Dead? Somehow, through our tears, by His grace we responded. "Yes, Lord. You may have them; they are yours. We love you."

For a week they were dead to us. Helicopters brought missionary refugees to the little town of Kikwit, people who had lost everything but their lives. I will never forget the Catholic nuns. They came off the aircraft and threw their arms around our necks, sobbing out their story of terror. Their priests had been hacked to pieces with machetes; their buildings were burned until the corrugated aluminum roofing had melted and hung down like giant icicles over the stone walls.

"Will you look for our family?" we petitioned the Canadian major in charge of the rescue operation. With the discipline born of soldiery he turned sad eyes upon us.

"I'm sorry," he said. "Your family is dead. I'm willing to die looking for the living, but not for the dead."

With that he pulled a flashlight from his hip pocket and handed it to me. "Look at it. See the hole in the end of the battery compartment? Now take the lens and reflector off."

There, nestled against the bulb was the bullet which had passed through the floor of the UN helicopter when it had been fired upon from the ground.

"That flashlight was in my back pocket. The bullet which would have killed me was stopped by the batteries."

But later he relented, and approached us again. "If you'll draw me a map so we can survey the Iwungu station, we'll take a look."

It was late in the day, but an independent pilot with his single prop airplane offered to make a survey trip right then. Darrell quickly scribbled a note on a cloth strip that could be dropped from the plane above the Iwungu station, alerting them to be prepared for evacuation the following morning.

The next morning we watched as three helicopters and a couple of aircraft equipped with rockets lifted off the airstrip and headed toward Iwungu. The dark specks disappeared over the horizon, and we waited with hearts in our throats.

Then, out of the blue, the helicopter specks returned. They hovered and began lowering to the ground. Finally, they were down!

We watched with bated breath, almost afraid to look, as the rotors spun to a stop and the doors opened...

Our loved ones began climbing out!

"All right," said our God. "You gave them to me; now you can have them back."

God had wonderfully watched over our family, for they had been able to retrieve the crucial note.[4] Norma, nine months in Congo, had seen God in a way in which she could never have seen Him otherwise. As Louise gathered little Deborah into her arms, having had the helicopter ride of her life, she exclaimed in surprise, "Mommy! Why are you crying?" Dad and Mom, having lived through the uncertainty of the ominous report that their children were dead, now had to realize these children were coming off an exciting ride—and for the moment, at least, they were no longer thinking of the ordeal of their Simba captivity.

The story of their rescue was told and retold. The fighter planes had come first, roaring so low over the trees that mangoes were knocked to the ground. The helicopters then dropped in, landing in spots we had indicated on our map. Soldiers leaped out, scanning the area with automatic weapons. The rebels fled into the surrounding brush, and the captive missionaries, including a priest, dashed to the helicopters and were up and out, a total of seventeen persons. A

---

4   View the actual note on the last page of the Photo Gallery, pg. 140.

testimony to the true heart of the Canadian officers and pilots became obvious when it was discovered a young Congolese girl who had been hiding was left behind, and they returned especially for her.

What a Godsend was the American ambassador who arrived in his twin engine Lockheed Electra. Having come to survey the catastrophic scene from the air, he was prepared to evacuate American citizens. Thus it was that we were lifted out of Kikwit in the ambassador's plane and deposited in Kinshasa, the capital. There we were lodged in UN barracks and fed on their rations. All the possessions we had left in the world fit in a couple of little metal trunks, but it was wonderful just to be together again, alive.[5]

With our jungle ministry in flames, destitute of both the opportunity and capability of continuing in Congo, we returned temporarily to the USA. Bob and Winifred needed to visit Jerome, Idaho to comfort Winifred's parents after the death of their daughter, Irene. All of us needed to re-equip ourselves for the future.

Somehow, word of our rescue had not reached my family in Salt Lake City, and they were mourning our deaths. When I telephoned from New York and said "Hi!", my brother's first words were, "Challenge you to a wrestle!" We had often wrestled as boys, he and I, for fun. I had won the last one. That was our welcome home. Once again, our sovereign and omnipotent God had proved His faithfulness.

"Yea, though I walk through the valley of the shadow of death, I will fear no evil: for thou art with me; thy rod and thy staff they comfort me. Thou preparest a table before me in the presence of mine enemies: thou anointest my head with oil; my cup runneth over." (Psalm 23:4–5)

5   Editor's note: It is well worth listening to the author
relate this story in his audio sermon, "Love With Shoes On".

ABDUCTED BY DRUNKEN SOLDIERS

Editor's note: This story occurs while the Champlins were waiting in Kinshasa for a flight back to the States, after the evacuation from their home station as described in the previous story.

An East Indian doctor and his doctor wife had lived in Kinshasa, capital of the Republic of Congo, for almost twenty years. Of their daughters, one was already practicing medicine in India and a second was studying in the USA. The parents had decided their patience with Congo was about used up and their income was being decimated by unjust and outlandish taxes. It was time to say goodbye to old friends and Congo. We were visiting in Kinshasa at the time and staying at the dismal little apartment rented by Bob and Winifred Grings behind some stores in downtown Kinshasa. We decided to walk a number of blocks through the center of town to the doctors' home; the streets were dirty and cluttered due to the virtual absence of any garbage collection service. The city was not a safe place to walk about late at night.

At ten o'clock it was time to head back to Bob's place. "Let us give you a ride," the doctor suggested. Not wanting to bother them, we declined the offer. Little did we know what would follow that fateful decision.

Leaving the house, we walked out into the almost-deserted streets of downtown Kinshasa, a sprawling city of perhaps four million. Rats as big as cats scurried in the gutters and between the crowded houses. Dogs barked here and there, and a pall of smoke hung over the city created by the little trash fires set by each of the store sentries from the trash they gathered in front of their stores before wrapping in a blanket and going to sleep across the doorway. Few vehicles could be heard moving on the mishmash of streets running at all angles. Here and there a person or two could be seen wandering in the dim glow of the city lights. We worked our way through the streets, angling always in the direction of Bob's quarters. We were within a block or two of home when we met them.

The soldiers were harassing a Congolese national in loud, half-drunken voices. Poorly paid, these soldiers made up for the money shortage by stopping vehicles during the day and charging them for ridiculous violations—headlights of a different brand, tires of a different make, scratches or dents on a fender. There was no appeal, no rule of law. Drivers paid the fines and left, muttering under their breaths and hoping not to be stopped by another group of policemen or soldiers. Most did not carry their driver's licenses because it was cheaper to pay for being caught without it than to buy back a license once the soldiers or police got it in their hands. So the national was having a hard time with the soldiers, alone in a deserted street.

Then they turned toward us. We could read their thoughts on their faces: "Aha, some real victims tonight, how nice." They shouted at us to come over to them.

"Where are your passports?" they demanded. "How come you are out so late at night? You are under arrest." They marched us off at gunpoint. Stopping to search us, they found no wallet, no passports, and no money. Louise had some family pictures in her purse, which they snatched.

"Who is this, and this, and this?" they asked. Ludicrous, half-drunken questions—but with a hint of cunning. They were going to abuse us into giving them all the money we had, if they could find any.

With their AK-47s at our backs they marched us through the gate of a ten-foot steel stake fence. As we passed I called to sentries in front of a Portuguese store. "Look at what these soldiers are doing to us; tell your white men to call the police."

"Ha, what will the police do?" laughed the soldiers. They pushed us back into an alcove that looked like a worker's lunch area. "Sit there on that bench," they ordered. One soldier sat at the end of the bench, the commanding officer stood over us.

"You're spies," he declared.

"Would spies be able to speak Lingala as we do?" we countered.

"You speak old Lingala," they retorted.

"All the more reason to prove we are not spies. What spies could speak old Lingala?"

"Where is your money? Where do you have it hidden? Give us money." On it went for an hour.

"Take his shoes off," the commanding officer ordered his inferior. But the fellow wasn't strong enough to do it.

"We'll separate you," they decided. "My man will take your wife to her brother's house, and I'll keep you here."

"No," I flatly refused. "You will not separate us."

"We'll separate you when you go to jail," the commander retorted.

"Take us then," I demanded.

On this went until I told them simply, "The God of Heaven is not pleased with what you are doing with us, and I am going to talk with Him about it."

"No, you cannot pray," he shouted. But I bowed my head and began to pray in his language telling God of their abuse.

"No!" he commanded and began to hit my head with his rifle.

For a while they calmed down, but then the pace began to pick up once more. Again I told them I was going to pray. This time they were quiet and at the end said, "Amen."

"Okay, we'll take you to your brother to get some money. Let's go."

We started off, their guns still leveled at our backs. We were almost to the corner when they called out again.

"Stop! Do not go around that corner."

I called back without looking, "You said you were taking us to my wife's brother, and we are going there." I knew what to expect when we rounded the corner. Immediately, the alarmed store sentries came running toward us. All of them knew us from the evening Bible devotions we held with them before they laid down for the night in front of their store entryways.

"What are these soldiers doing to you?" they questioned with great agitation and reproach against the soldiers. At that moment two Portuguese businessmen pulled up beside us in their Mercedes Benz (the men I was referring to when I had shouted across the street to their sentries, "Tell your white men.").

Now we had an escort taking us down the street to Bob's house. He came out in his pajamas, having gone to bed at midnight. After much discussion with the soldiers he gave them some money and gospel tracts, and they went on their nefarious way.

Once again, we had found our God to be a present, prayer-answering God in the midst of danger and disreputable soldiers. It was with very thankful hearts we slipped into our beds under the mosquito nets that night.

"God is our refuge and strength, a very present help in trouble." (Psalm 46:1)

BIMA! BIMA!

IRENE FERREL

The Portuguese explorer Diego Cam discovered the mouth of the Congo river in 1482. Slave trade developed and flourished there until the 19th century. Then in the early 1800s, exploration of the interior culminated in Henry Stanley's historic pioneer trip down the length of Congo in 1886–1887. King Leopold II of Belgium, with a long held view favoring expansion into Africa, was ultimately granted sovereignty over Congo in 1885 by the European powers in conference at Berlin, Germany. The inauguration of the Congo Free State, ruled by King Leopold II, was declared on July 1, 1885.

Thus began the export of ivory and rubber, which netted rich revenues for Leopold and the large private companies to which he granted monopoly privileges. However, the use of forced labor and the restriction of free trade led to such protests against Leopold's rule from the rest of the western world that in 1908, Belgium formally annexed the Free State and it became the Belgian Congo. In 1919 Belgium acquired a League of Nations mandate over the former German possession of Ruanda-Urundi.

Great strides were made in the development of the territories.

The Congo River and its tributaries give Congo the best waterways in Africa, with 8500 miles of rivers that are navigable year-round. Besides the waterways, 86,000 miles of roads were developed, 1,000 of them paved. An interior air travel network of 22,000 miles was also put in place, the most extensive in all of Africa. Almost all of the educational facilities were placed in the hands of the missionaries, some 10,000 in number at their peak, most of them Roman Catholic. Hospitals, clinics, rural dispensaries, and ninety-nine treatment centers for leprosy, sleeping sickness and tuberculosis also helped to raise the African standard of living considerably further beyond what they could have ever imagined.

However, an Achilles heel was lurking in an otherwise pleasant situation. Political pressure from around the world was growing on Belgium to grant independence to Congo. The two Congo universities housed a total of 546 students, and the population of fourteen million counted few university graduates in its number. No elections were held until 1957, then numerous political parties sprang up, principally based along tribal lines, of which there are over two hundred in Congo. Now a cry went up from the tribes demanding immediate independence. In 1959, rioting and major outbursts of violence in the capital, Léopoldville, and other parts of Congo led the Belgian government to grant premature independence on June 30, 1960. From this point Congo spiraled downward into utter chaos.

To this country had come a farm girl born in South Dakota. Irene Ferrel had lost her mother at eleven and moved with her family the following year, 1936, to Filer, Idaho. After Bible School in Los Angeles, she was called to the mission field during a summer camp. Her ship docked at Matadi, one hundred miles up the Congo River, on August 25, 1951; and with two other young women she stepped off into her mission field. Her sister Winifred, already on the field, married Robert Grings in December of that same year, thus inextricably linking the Grings' and Ferrels' lives. Bessie Grings, Bob and Louise's sister, was one of the young ladies who came to the field with Irene that August.

Years of fruitful service passed. Irene was a natural athlete, and flourished both in the outdoors life of jungle evangelism as well as in the service of the mission station and skills of a homemaker. Before her last furlough however, a collapsed lung was diagnosed, revealing precarious health. Doctors performed surgery in America to restore the lung. Advised by some to stay in the USA, she responded, "My Lord has not instructed me to stay in the USA but rather to return to the field," and again she departed for her beloved Africa.

Congo was in a state of great discontent. Unrealistic Congolese politicians had promised the people that independence would mean no work, no responsibility, no struggle, no taxes, and truck loads of money. Paved roads, large homes, automobiles, bicycles, food, and clothing—all free, all part of this glorious thing called "Independence." Even the dead would rise. This shocking news had set off the clearing of burial plots and paths leading back to the villages so the dead could easily find their way. We had watched in amazement and tried to reason with them, but the answer was always, "What do you know about it? When did a white man ever get independence?"

But now discontent began to bubble, then flood across the country. There was no work; 900% inflation roared across the land. Independence was a bust. "Let's give our independence back to the Belgians," became the theme of many a mind and heart. The stage was set for revolution against the new black government.

Onto this stage stepped Mulele Pierre, trained as an insurgent by his Marxist mentors in Peking for the express purpose of fomenting a rebellion to bring down the weak, newly formed, disorganized black African government and installing a Marxist regime. By 1964 a wildfire of destruction was sweeping the nation. Murder, rape, pillaging, and plunder ravaged the countryside as the Simbas began their gruesome march. Mulele Pierre's home village was but nineteen miles from the mission station of Mangungu staffed by Ruth Hege, Irene Ferrel, and their national coworkers.

The undisciplined, ill-trained Congolese army did little to improve the situation. In their drive to capture Mulele Pierre, they too looted, raped, and killed innocent civilians. Young girls fled to the mission outposts for protection from the rapacious soldiers. Rumors filled the land that bullets could not affect the witchcraft-protected Simbas. A village chief and teachers from a nearby village were dragged from their houses, beaten, and hacked to death. Irene and Ruth were surrounded by the surging violence, but with typical old-fashioned missionary disdain for danger, they carried on.

In fact, we met as usual for our new year's family gathering. This group included Bob and Winifred Grings and their children, Mark Grings, Wyla Weekly, a nurse who would later become Mark's wife; Louise, myself, our children, Norma Jenkins, Irene Ferrel, and Ruth Hege. It was a close-knit group at peace with each other and their God, surrounded by a nation exploding. As we monitored the short wave missionary broadcasts we learned that the mission station at Kafumba had been invaded and razed. The situation was indeed serious.

On the morning of January 13, Irene and Ruth left the Grings' station at Iwungu with confidence and assurance that God was leading back to their station, Mangungu. Twelve days later the storm broke.

The thunder of bare running feet stampeded through the midnight darkness toward Irene and Ruth's house. The station guards cried out in fear and anger as thirty or forty drug and alcohol-crazed Simbas filled the air with spine-chilling shrieks. Glass flew as the windows were shattered. Ruth awoke, dressed quickly, and met Irene coming from the bathroom, fully dressed. She hadn't gone to bed yet.

"*Bima! Bima! Bima!* (Get out, get out, get out!)" screamed the Simbas as they burst into the house waving burning grass torches and brandishing bows, arrows, and long sharp knives. They dragged and pushed the two women from the house, tearing their clothing. In a frenzy they thrust Irene and Ruth down the steps.

An arrow flashed out of the darkness and pierced Irene's neck with terrible force. Blood fountained as Irene pulled the arrow from her throat and dropped lifeless to the ground. Ruth, covered by Irene's blood and her own from an arrow wound to the shoulder, fell beside her and lost consciousness.

As the looting and razing of the property continued, Ruth came to while trembling violently, sensing footsteps approaching. *Oh God, what would movement on her part incite?* God's hand upon her stilled the trembling, and calmness took its place. Twice a Simba put his hand on her side; twice he was satisfied she was dead. Another came by and yanked out a lock of her hair to wear as a strength-giving fetish.

"*Fwa* (dead)!" was their verdict, and they left her. The schoolhouse was now burning from end to end, its eerie light illuminating frantic figures carrying off their booty.

When things quieted, Ruth painfully arose and made her way to the little bamboo-walled, thatch-roofed garage where she found a couple bags of cracked wheat and beans. Dumping the contents on the garage floor, she lay down and covered herself with the burlap bags. At last, she slept. Irene's body lay where she had fallen.

Faithful Christians found Ruth in the morning with crimson-smeared face, clot-caked hair, and blood-stained clothes. Lovingly they cared for her, and she was able to assist in the burial of Irene's body. Apprehended again by the rebels, she was miraculously rescued by UN helicopters several days later, and preserved for further service to her God.[1] As for Irene, what a glorious promotion into the presence of her Lord and Savior to receive His "Well done, thou good and faithful servant, enter thou into the joy of thy Lord." One of whom the world was not worthy!

Our thoughts draw us to II Corinthians 5:1–8. "For we know that if our earthly house of this tabernacle were dissolved, we have a building of God, an house not made with hands, eternal in the heavens. For in this we groan, earnestly desiring to be clothed upon with our house which is from heaven: If so be that being clothed we shall not be found naked. For we that are in this tabernacle do groan, being burdened: not for that we would be unclothed, but clothed upon, that mortality might be swallowed up of life. Now he that hath wrought us for the selfsame thing is God, who also hath given unto us the earnest of the Spirit. Therefore we are always confident, knowing that, whilst we are at home in the body, we are absent from the Lord: (For we walk by faith, not by sight:) We are confident, I say, and willing rather to be absent from the body, and to be present with the Lord."

---

1   She went on to write "We Two Alone: Attack and Rescue in the Congo" (Emerald House Group, 1998) which provides a full account of this period.

Editor's note: *Irene Ferrel was the first of thirty missionaries to give their lives as martyrs during the Simba Revolution. Well-known among this number is Dr. Paul Carson, who was shot to death along with four other missionaries in Kisangani. His story was featured in both Time and Life magazines, his wife wrote his biography "Monganga Paul", and the Evangelical Covenant Church produced his story as a documentary, "Monganga".*

BEARING THE INIQUITY

A subject seldom considered or even discovered by God's people is the principle of *"bearing the iniquity"*. There comes a time in the history of a nation that its iniquity (which I define as an accumulation of wickedness, a fulminating of unrighteousness, and a promulgation of satanic sinfulness) demands judgment. The Apostle Paul expresses it in Romans 1:32: "Who knowing the judgment of God, that they which commit such things are worthy of death, not only do the same, but have pleasure in them that do them." They are against whom "the wrath of God is revealed from heaven." (Romans 1:18)

Ezekiel's people, the impudent, stiff-hearted, and rebellious Israel, were under the judgment of God (Ezekiel 2:3–4). Ezekiel was made a watchman unto the house of Israel to warn them of impending doom (Ezekiel 3:17). King Zedekiah had rebelled against Nebuchadnezzar, the King of Babylon, making Nebuchadnezzar furious. So horrible would be the siege laid against Israel that mothers would boil and eat their own children (Lamentations 4:10).

However, Ezekiel was responsible not only to warn his people of the horrors to come, but also to go with them through the judgment

273

(Ezekiel 4). He was to bear their iniquity, which means that he was to join God in His judgment of the people's sin, and to join the people in the destitution brought to pass by the judgment of God. In summary, his task was to warn the people that God was going to judge them, and to go with them through the judgment.

Ezekiel 4:1–3 commands Ezekiel to set his face against the sin of his people. Verses 4–5 command Ezekiel to bear the iniquity of his people—going through the judgment with them. This entailed living with them in the disaster brought on by their sin; staying with them in spite of *and* because of the destruction of their bodies by the fruits of their idolatry and debauchery. Living with the blind, broken, bewildered, and bereft. Loving their souls in spite of their wantonness, the pornography of their hearts, their eyes, and their mouths. Holding them and hugging them in his heart.

Ezekiel 4:5 declares, "For I have laid upon thee the years of their iniquity...three hundred and ninety days: so shalt thou bear the iniquity of the house of Israel."

You see this principle exemplified in Moses in Exodus 32:30–32, where he cries out "...if thou wilt forgive their sin—; and if not, blot me, I pray thee, out of Thy book."

Again we see it in Paul in Romans 9:3; "For I could wish that myself were accursed from Christ for my brethren, my kinsmen according to the flesh."

The most remarkable illustration of this principle's application is that of our Lord Jesus Christ as described in Isaiah 53:4–7: "Surely he hath borne our griefs, and carried our sorrows: yet we did esteem him stricken, smitten of God, and afflicted. But he was wounded for our transgressions, he was bruised for our iniquities: the chastisement of our peace was upon him; and with his stripes we are healed. All we like sheep have gone astray; we have turned every one to his own way; and the Lord hath laid on him the iniquity of us all."

You might ask, "How far does the servant of God go in bearing the iniquity of his people?"

The answer is in Ezekiel 4:14–15: "I have given thee cow's dung for man's dung". How far does the servant of God go in staying with his people, sharing the judgment which has fallen upon them? The answer is—anything but sin.

This willingness to bear the iniquity of their people characterized such prophets as Jeremiah, Isaiah, and Elijah. The Apostles all walked in the footsteps of their Master, giving their lives by going through the same persecution which slaughtered their fellow Christians. Old-fashioned missionaries, thousands of whose bodies fertilized Africa and Asia, followed in their train. Many died within months of their arrival on the fields; few in China between the years of 1900 and 1960 celebrated more than forty birthdays. During one long period of early Eastern Africa pioneer outreach, the longest span of service was sixteen years; the average was eight. These old time missionaries went to the field not expecting ever to return. Bearers of the iniquity of their people, they were true representatives of the Lamb of God upon Whom our iniquities were laid.

Bob and Winifred Grings bring our subject up into the 1990s. For years they lived in the jungles, suffering with their primitive people the privations of life in the heart of Congo, Africa. Their housing would have been comparable to a normal chicken coop in the States. Their meager diet, bereft of all the choices common to and demanded by our American society, left Bob so thin I joked with him that he disappeared when he turned sideways. Wracked by malaria again and again, drained by dysentery, scarred by fungi, eaten internally

275

by worms, they lived with their people in the people's circumstances. I smile when I hear folks express the idea that veteran missionaries have somehow escaped the diseases and physical hardships inherent to tropical ministries. The fact of the matter is that they have had the diseases and are still there. Your writer and his wife are two of them.

When, at last, the Grings' responsibilities forced them to move to the capital city, Kinshasa, you would have thought their life would have experienced what might be called an "upgrade". But, no. Their financial straits, due to years of continuous service without sufficient furlough breaks to raise additional support and their ongoing practice of continuous giving, made it necessary to find cheap lodging downtown. A long, narrow apartment, it was situated behind and between store buildings. Blocked on four sides with only a narrow driveway giving access to the filthy street, it sweltered in the tropical heat with little ventilation. One entered the property and encountered a kind of dirt plaza where little open fires burned as stragglers prepared poor meals. Drugs and alcohol were evident everywhere. The business transacted there would not be edifying to elucidate here. In the evening, a pall of smoke arose throughout the neighborhood as the sentries (hired by stores to sleep across their doorways through the night) gathered trash from in front of their stores and burned it. Many such fires winked through the haze of the early evening all over the massive city of four million. Bob Grings made a practice of having evening devotions with these sentries from up and down the street.

The apartment was actually a duplex. The other end was occupied by an African family. Various visitors were in and out throughout the day, both to Bob and Winifred's apartment and to their African neighbors'. What diseases were represented one can only guess. The fact that the government of Congo admitted to the horror that one million of the four million inhabitants of Kinshasa were HIV positive gave pause when we realized that only one toilet and shower served both apartments. That this did not disturb Bob and Winifred was evident, the reason being that it would not have disturbed their Lord, His prophets, His Apostles, or His great old time missionaries.

Winifred has since gone to be with her Lord and heard His "Well done, thou good and faithful servant." Bob continues in Congo, and at eighty-eight is as skinny as ever. Still riding his bicycle over both jungle trails and the cluttered, chaotic streets of Kinshasa. Still eating, with apparent relish, the grubs, monkey meat, and cassava leaves served to him by his beloved nationals. Still wading the swamps of the forest and the incredible trash of a city where there has been no regular collection of garbage for thirty years. Still sorrowing with the broken-hearted, sympathizing with the bereft, and singing with the joyful. Still taking every opportunity to reach a soul for Christ, whether in an office, on a street corner, from a pulpit—or helping dig a vehicle out of a mud hole big enough to swallow a truck up to the steering wheel. Still being what he is, an extraordinary bearer of the iniquity of his people. He is unconscious of the fact that it is strange to some people. His own people are saying of him, "We have never had another missionary like him," and asking "Will we ever see another?"

Will we see another from an America which finds the subject of *"bearing the iniquity"* strange and unfamiliar? I wonder. From you, reader? From your home, your family? Perhaps?

FIRST PLACE OR EVERYTHING?
THE EICHERS

The Eichers lived at Balaka, a village located in the vast rolling hills and grasslands of Congo. Dirt roads crisscrossed the area, dipping deep into the valleys where little forests (*ipoka*) grew and climbing again to the broad expanse of the plains. The Bayaka people lived in large villages of grass-roofed round huts dotting the plains and smaller ones nestled in the valleys. Partridges and grassland guinea fowl, gray feathered with white spots in contrast to their blue-feathered white-spotted jungle cousins, could be seen in the mornings. Bustards, the long-legged, long-necked, wild chickens of the grasslands melted into the dry grasses with their speckled brown feathers. Turkey-sized King Bustards, swift and alert, strode through the more remote areas where human beings were not so frequently seen. Jackals roamed in pairs, seeking rodents and ground nesting birds such as quail, and chasing down newborn *nse*, a light brown-jacketed, white-shirted antelope the size of a goat.

Alas, the grown antelope were too alert and far too swift to be caught. Majestic *nkai*, the bush buck, came out of the valley forests to feed on the tender shoots of the burned off plains. The *kabaji*, far larger than the bush buck, stood outlined against the horizon in the setting sun, horns towering to the sky, shoulders horse high. The hunter fortunate enough to spot one of these elusive beasts and skillful enough to bring one down could feed more than a hundred people with its meat. Once, I shot one myself from several hundred yards away as it stood up at the moment when the sun slipped down and the afterglow reflected beautifully off the clouds.

The civet cat is dog-like in that its claws do not retract, cat-like in face and fur, and skunk-like in its musky, unpleasant odor. It would skulk around the villages for the opportunity to steal a chicken or munch on someone's pineapples. Unsuccessful in that pursuit, he would search for ground nesting birds and eat various wild fruits. The *lokagna* (you would call them crows) cawed in their raucous voices at those who had disturbed their peace—or just to caw. It was Africa—an Africa beyond the imagination of those who have only seen pictures of it.

Auguste and Helene Eicher were Swiss missionaries who loved Africa and the Bayaka. To a young missionary of twenty-two, the Eichers looked old. They were in their fifties, at least, when I first met them. Strangely, I write this story at sixty-eight and don't feel old. It's a matter of perspective, I guess.

I remember being chased out of their outdoor pit latrine by fierce black wasps, great stings swelling on my head and swimming in pain. Beyond this I knew little about Balaka, or even the Eichers except for the fact that they were brave, real missionaries.

Auguste Eicher was the legal representative for his mission, and his eyes were so poor he had to hold a book up close to read it with his thick glasses. Also of note is the fact that he had done great service, not only in the preaching of the Gospel but also through helping people with medical treatment, as he had been trained to some degree in medicine. Especially was this the case in the scourge of venereal diseases that had spread through the villages. Evidence abounded that they loved their people and their God in an extraordinary way.

That became unmistakably plain when the Simba rebels swept through their area and stormed into their house. Driving Mr. and Mrs. Eicher to their knees, the rebels stood over them and demanded, "If you do not deny this Jesus, we will kill you!" Looking fearlessly into the rebels' wild faces, the couple declared, "You may kill us, but we will never deny our Lord."

With that, the Simbas jerked Auguste to his feet and thrust him out the door. Helene, standing in the living room could hear the Christians crying, "Don't do that, don't do that." A soft, firm *thud, thud, thud* echoed into the house; they were beating Auguste with a twelve-pound sledge hammer.

He was more dead than alive when national Christians were able to rescue the Eichers; they were hidden in the forest for nine days. After the death of Irene Ferrel, helicopters searching for survivors snatched Ruth Hege from the clutches of the rebels when they spotted her being secretly pushed on a bicycle by a faithful old village man. Aided by information from national Christians, the helicopters continued their sweep until they located and rescued the Eichers. They were flown to Switzerland, where by the grace of God Auguste recovered.

About a year later, we met the Eichers at Grace Baptist Church in Belleville, Michigan. What a glorious time of fellowship we had, and what a wonderful testimony we heard. The Eichers were making plans to return to Congo. And return they did, right back to the place where they had knelt with machetes raised over their heads. Back to the place where the Simbas had beaten Auguste with a sledgehammer.

281

Back to the Bayaka people whom they loved, flawed as they were. Back for the God they loved.

Does that sound like giving God "first place"? Sounds more to me like utter abandonment in love to the majestic God of the universe. It sounds not like first place, but like everything. Not priority, but authority; real missionaries living Biblically. God have mercy upon the peoples of the world by giving them more missionaries like the Eichers.

"I beseech you therefore, brethren, by the mercies of God, that ye present your bodies a living sacrifice, holy, acceptable unto God... that ye my prove what is that good, and acceptable, and perfect, will of God." (Romans 12:1, 2.)

BOWS AND ARROWS AGAINST AUTOMATIC WEAPONS

Editor's note: This story occurs in the year following the Champlins' evacuation. Louise writes, "Our first visit back in 1988 gave us the opportunity to talk with the survivors and get the tales of the soldiers' invasion and ruthless activities. We did receive some information about our Nkole Nkema station soon after our evacuation via a pilot that had flown over. He described the destruction scene as though a feather pillow had been emptied on the lawn scattering our books, dishes, furnishings, and other belongings. The tin roof of our house had been removed and the building set on fire. There was nothing left to go back to. We accepted it in the spirit of Romans 12:1, a "living sacrifice", and to "not be overcome with evil, but overcome evil with good." The Christian village was also destroyed at the same time, so folks had to hide deep in the jungle where the invading army was unfamiliar and unable to capture or kill them."
This scene of mayhem and violence provides the backdrop for the following story.

If a war was fought between soldiers armed with automatic weapons and people armed with bows and arrows, who would you expect to win? You might be surprised to learn that such a war was won, and which side was victorious—especially if you were to meet them face to face and hear their incredible story, as I have. That is the story I relate to you on these pages.

It was the late 1960s and the situation in the land of Congo was desperate. Nowhere was life more at risk than in the Boldi area among the Bankutu people. The villages were now but cinders; thirteen churches had been burned to the ground and seven schools lay in ruins. Twenty of the thirty-six preachers who had served them had been murdered. The people were in the jungle hiding for their lives, for soldiers had entered their area in pursuit of the Simba rebels who had laid much of the country to waste.

In the beginning it had looked as though the Simbas would overthrow the newly independent black government. The Republic of Congo gained independence on June 30, 1960 after having been ruled by Belgium since July 1, 1885. But the country was torn by internal strife and the government was weak. Marxist-trained insurgents, being used by their Communist mentors to bring Congo into their sphere, terrified the army with fetish-festooned spears and bows and arrows. The army believed such warriors could not be killed by bullets, and often threw down their automatic weapons and fled before these charging banshees. At last the discovery was made that the charms and fetishes of the rebels did not protect them from bullets, and with that the tide of battle began to turn. Now the Simba Revolution was nearly over, at last burning itself out against the heavily armed Congo soldiery.

From the vengeful heart of the President came an ill-conceived and ill-informed order to annihilate the Bankutu people of our area in the deep interior of Congo. He blamed them with having aided the

284

rebels, and determined upon genocide as punishment. Thus it was that Congolese soldiers stayed in our area, already devastated by the war, for the purpose of the complete destruction of our people. Encamping themselves in our house, the church, and the houses of our mission station, the army began a systematic sweep of the jungle trails with the intent of killing every Bankutu tribesman they could find.

Our people were cut off from their gardens where they would ordinarily dig cassava, harvest the leaves for vegetables, cut bunches of bananas and plantains, and pick ripe pineapples scattered here and there among the other plants. Sweet potatoes, too, could be had in season. Now the soldiers plundered their gardens and lay in ambush waiting for the owners to sneak from their hiding places in the jungle to find something to eat. Hunger grew and starvation began to take its toll.

Meanwhile, scouting patrols sought out our people, who built only crude stick and palm branch shelters in their constantly moving camps. Those who were found by the soldiers were shot, or sometimes taken back and tortured. Perpetually moving was the only way our people could survive. Fortunately, they were thoroughly familiar with the jungle, and the soldiers were not. Months dragged by and the people's trusted apostle, Pastor Bekanga Paul, lay dying of a fulminating boil on the side of his neck.[1] He called the men together and presented the urgent question: "Elijah is going to glory. Who will be the Elisha to take his mantle?" Ilonga Petelo, his brother-in-law, assumed that great responsibility of leadership. The situation was growing increasingly desperate. At last our people made a fateful decision. "If we

---

1 Bekanga had been captured by soldiers prior to this, after which he lived in hiding in the jungles with his people. See "Lulu Bekanga" pg. 47, and "Ilonga Petelo", pg. 51, for the rest of this story.

continue to run we will all eventually be killed or die of disease and starvation. We must fight!"

Fight? With bows and arrows against automatic weapons? Fight weak with hunger and disease against well-fed soldiers? Our people had one modern gun in their possession, my .30-06 bolt action rifle, and a cache of cartridges taken from our house during the Simba fighting. And they had one man, an old soldier, who knew how to shoot it. So it was that he began to lay ambush for the soldiers, waiting until he could get two or three of them standing in a row, and then *Makalele Monene* spoke, seemingly out of nowhere. Thus, with that gun he created a "terror of the jungle".

Then our people discovered that automatic weapon fire usually starts about knee high and swings upward with the torque of the weapon. They took to approaching the soldiers by crawling on their stomachs until they were within range and then, on signal, rising as one to loose a hail of arrows. Down on their stomachs again, moving like snakes, they waited until the frantic soldiers had exhausted their clips firing wildly, and then rose again to let loose another hail of arrows. We laughed and cried as our people described these battles, crawling on their stomachs in demonstration of how the battles were waged.

Battle after battle was won, until one day they went out with two hundred and sixty-eight men and returned having lost sixty-eight! Sitting in broken-hearted gloom, they pondered the reason. Then it became clear. Hunger was so terrible that Christians had begun to steal from each other. The sin of Achan was in the camp! Falling on their faces in repentance, they rose with the forgiveness of God and His power once more upon them.

Slipping stealthily out of the jungle, brave individuals set fire to our house, the church, and many of the houses in the Christian village which were being occupied by the soldiers. The smoke rising from these buildings signaled the beginning of the end for the soldiers. In recognition that these benighted jungle people armed with bows and arrows and a single terrifying gun evidently had the prospering of a Super Power and were gaining the upper hand, the soldiers petitioned their president for permission to leave. In effect, they now feared annihilation for themselves, rather than for the Bankutu people.

Miraculously, the soldiers had lost a war against a foe armed only with bows and arrows. So it was that, when the soldiers began to decamp, Ilonga Petelo walked into the soldiers' camp and announced that the Christians were taking possession.

A sergeant shouted, "I'll shoot him!" but the commanding officer intervened.

"No, we were whipped by an army equipped with bows and arrows *and God*, and I accept His authority. The place is yours, sir."

Thus ended an incredible war, and the Sovereignty and Power of the God of Heaven was demonstrated once again.

"With God all things are possible." (Matthew 19:26b)

"Behold, I am the Lord, the God of all flesh: is there anything too hard for me?" (Jeremiah 32:27)

EPILOGUE

LOUISE CHAMPLIN, JULY 2017

The Simba Revolution of 1964 in Congo necessitated our family's evacuation back to the United States where we sought the Lord's direction. God led us in mid-1965 to our next mission field in Suriname, South America. Although it was a different continent, we were working with descendants of tribal groups among whom we had ministered in Congo.

In 1988, Darrell and I made a return visit to Congo where we found that the churches and schools we had planted had amazingly come up out of the ashes, been rebuilt, and were going on for the Lord. We visited periodically during the following years, encouraging and supporting the believers in their faith.

Starting in 1977, we began representing Independent Faith Mission part-time. This meant returning to the States each year where we spoke at various churches and Bible colleges. At first it was just the two months before Thanksgiving, deemed as the best time to present college seniors with mission challenges. Eventually, the requests became too numerous to fit in a two-month period, so we began making two trips each year in the spring and the fall.

Summer and winter months were still spent in Suriname. It was during these months that Darrell sat at his desk and created the rough drafts from which this book was created. His enduring memories and inimitable writing style have brought these stories to vivid life for all who will read them.

"Love With Shoes On" is Darrell's best known message, one that spread around the globe and which God powerfully used to impact thousands with a passion for missions, a God-sent question echoing in their minds: "*How* do you love Me?" Darrell's life proved a resounding answer: "I love You, *with shoes on.*"

On August 26, 2015, Darrell quietly passed away in Suriname and was buried in the jungle where he had lived, labored, and loved. He left a legacy of faithful service and sacrificial love of his Lord, best expressed in the words of Borden of Yale:

"NO RESERVES. NO RETREATS. NO REGRETS."